RADICAL RENEWAL

RADICAL RENEWAL

by Luis Palau

CROSSWAY BOOKS

EASTBOURNE

ISBN 1 85684 044 2

Unless otherwise noted, Scripture quotations are from the Holy Bible:
New International Version, copyright © 1978 by the New York
International Bible Society. Other quotations are from the New
American Standard Bible (NASB), copyright © 1960, 1962, 1963, 1968,
and 1971 by the Lockman Foundation; from the New King James
Version (NKJV), copyright © 1982 by Thomas Nelson, Inc.; from the
Revised Standard Version of the Bible (RSV), copyright © 1946 and
1952 by the Division of Christian Education of the National Council of
Churches in the United States of America; and from The Living Bible
(TLB), © 1971 by Tyndale House Publishers.

The author has taken certain literary licence to protect the identity of
some of the individuals and families mentioned in this book.

Production and Printing in England for
CROSSWAY BOOKS
Glyndley Manor, Pevensey, Eastbourne, East Sussex BN24 5BS by
Nuprint Ltd, Station Road, Harpenden, Herts AL5 4SE

CONTENTS

ACKNOWLEDGEMENTS

My thanks to Ray Stedman, George Kehoe, Ian Thomas, Fred Renich, Albert Wollen, John Hunter, Ed Murphy, Eugenia Price, and the many others who were used of God to teach and reinforce the principles of radical renewal in my own life. And my deep gratitude to Patricia, my wife, whose love and honesty have encouraged me to grow still closer to the Lord.

My thanks to David Sanford for editing this book. It's been a pleasure to teach the principles of radical renewal on many occasions, but it took Dave's persistence to help make this book a reality. Dave is a respected friend of our family. I praise God for His servant attitude toward the Church and concern for those who have yet to trust Jesus Christ.

And my thanks to you for starting to read this book. My prayer is that you will stick with me for the next 153 pages, and that God will use the principles in this book to redirect and revitalize the whole course of your Christian experience.

ABOUT THE AUTHOR

Luis Palau stands out in this generation as a truly international Christian spokesman and leader. He's a third generation transplanted European who grew up in the province of Buenos Aires, Argentina, went to the United States to take the graduate course at Multnomah School of the Bible in Portland, Oregon, and now has become an evangelist to the world.

Equally at ease in English and Spanish, Luis Palau commands audiences' attention wherever he goes. His solidly biblical, practical messages hit home in the minds and hearts of listeners. 'Sometimes it seems I have been preaching all my life,' says Luis. 'Actually, although I started preaching in Argentina as a teenager, it really wasn't until I was in my thirties that God opened the door for me to pursue full-time mass evangelism.'

During the 1970s Luis and his team conducted evangelistic campaigns and rallies throughout Latin America. Invitations also started coming from Europe and other parts of the world. By the early 1980s, Luis Palau's ministry had taken Britain by storm and new doors were opening all around the globe.

Since then, huge crowds in countries as diverse as Argentina and Brazil, Colombia and Denmark, Guatemala and Hungary, Hong Kong and India, Indonesia and Japan, Mexico and New Zealand, Peru and Romania, Singapore and the Soviet Union, Thailand and the United States have packed out concert halls, arenas and stadiums to hear Luis Palau.

The impact? Hundreds of thousands of people have trusted

Jesus Christ and become established as disciples in local churches. Cities and nations have heard a clear-cut proclamation of the Gospel.

'Luis is probably more in demand among evangelicals to preach and speak than almost any other person in the world,' says Billy Graham. 'Wherever there is an evangelical conference they try to get Luis Palau, because he is a powerful preacher. But more than that, he is an evangelist that God has given a multiplicity of gifts to, and thousands of people come to hear him every year, and other thousands are won to Christ.'

To date, Luis Palau has proclaimed the Good News of Jesus Christ in person to nearly nine million people on six continents, and to many tens of millions through radio and television broadcasts in ninety-four countries.

In addition to his dynamic speaking ministry, Luis Palau is a prolific author. His twenty-nine books include the powerful *What Is a Real Christian?* evangelistic booklet, which has been published in thirty languages worldwide. Luis also has contributed articles to more than a dozen books and scores of periodicals.

Luis and his wife Pat, also a popular conference speaker and author, have served as missionary-evangelists in Colombia and Mexico. The Palaus have four grown sons and now make their home near the international headquarters of the Luis Palau Evangelistic Association.

INTRODUCTION

It isn't every day that Natasha, a Soviet journalist, finds herself interviewing a foreigner, let alone a Christian. She has worked hard to achieve her prominent position within the communist youth movement in the Soviet Union. She prides herself in her work as a reporter. But today's assignment was anything but typical.

To say the least, Natasha wasn't overly sympathetic to me or the message I was preaching during a five-city tour of her homeland. 'You don't look too happy,' I remarked at a particularly candid point toward the end of our interview.

'Of course not. We atheists are never happy,' Natasha retorted.

In a rather blunt way, Natasha's statement encapsulates the bankruptcy of denying God and biblical revelation. Atheism stifles the soul and kills the spirit. Suddenly there's no hope beyond ourselves. There's no future beyond the present. But as human beings, we have been created in the image of God. And even if we intellectually or emotionally deny Him, our souls cry out for spiritual reality.

Without God, life has no meaning, education has no purpose, economics has no direction. The many failed experiments of nationalized atheism in Eastern Europe should have proved that to this generation once and for all. The human soul clamours for God. No wonder a Christian revival appears to be sweeping countries like the Soviet Union and Romania.

This hunger is captured in a story a Baptist pastor told me in Leningrad. After Mikhail Gorbachev came to power, local Russian officials reopened an old Orthodox church building and turned it over to this pastor and his congregation. I visited the church building and it reminded me of pictures I've seen of buildings hit during the Nazi blitzkrieg in World War II. The ornate beauty of the church had long since been obliterated. Only the shell remains.

One day while working to fix up the inside of the church with a crew of men from Siberia, the Baptist pastor was interrupted by a man off the street. 'Is the priest here?'

'Yes, I'm the priest.' (There isn't a word in Russian for pastor.)

'There are four young ladies outside who want to talk to you.'

'Tell them to come in,' the pastor said.

'Oh, no. They don't want to come in. They refuse to come in.'

'All right, I'll come out.' So he walked out onto the street where the young women stood waiting for him. But when he stretched out his hand to greet them, they all refused the gesture.

'Why won't you shake my hand?'

'Are you a priest?' one of the young women asked.

'Yes, I am.'

'Well, we are not worthy to shake your hand.'

'Why not?'

'We are all prostitutes and the reason we've come and wanted to talk to you is to find out if God will ever forgive us for what we've done.'

'Of course He will forgive you!' The pastor took his Bible, opened it and told them about the death of Jesus Christ and the blood of Christ that cleanses from all sin.

'But would God ever forgive us for all the wicked things we've done?'

'If you receive Christ and invite Him into your life, of course He will forgive you.'

'Will He forgive us right now?'

'Yes, right now!' So there on the pavement the four women prayed with him to receive Jesus Christ. When they finished, one of the young women asked, 'Are we forgiven now?'

'Yes. You see the Bible says, 'Your sins and evil deeds I will remember no more. The blood of Jesus cleanses from all sin. So you are forgiven.'

Before this, the women wouldn't even shake the pastor's hand. Now they embraced him and asked, 'May we come into the church?' There wasn't much to see, but the pastor gave each young woman a Bible and explained more about what it means to experience God's forgiveness and receive new life in Christ. As the pastor told me this story, I was touched again by this fact: when they hear the Gospel of Christ, many people gladly embrace it. I find most people are painfully aware of their sinfulness. They're desperate for God's love and forgiveness. So when they hear the Gospel and receive Christ, the difference He makes in their lives is amazing for all to see.

One of my most rewarding experiences is meeting or receiving letters from men, women, and young people who have trusted Jesus Christ through our evangelistic campaigns, rallies and other outreaches. Sometimes years go by before I hear from them or meet them somewhere. But to hear their stories and find out what Christ has done in their lives is a great encouragement.

I received a letter today from one of the many thousands of people who made public decisions for Jesus Christ during our Mission to London evangelistic campaign at Queens Park Rangers stadium. The letter was written by someone who made a first-time commitment to Christ during the campaign. Interestingly, it was postmarked Bulawayo, Zimbabwe.

'I just thought I would write and let you know that one person from QPR 1984 is still going on for Jesus,' writes Valarie, who tells of 'six years of loving Jesus and being of service to Him' back home in southern Africa. Over the years

I've heard from hundreds of Valaries. I've kept all their letters as witnesses of the transforming power of the Gospel.

To look at some Christians, however, you have to wonder if they know anything about new life in Jesus Christ. Think about it. Have you met any fruitless, frustrated folks who don't seem to be enjoying the Christian life? I sure have.

Have you ever wondered if there is more—much more— to the Christian life than you've experienced so far? Have you ever dreamed about becoming a successful, fruitful, God-centered person?

Maybe you've sensed such a life is possible. You want to enjoy it. You're searching for it. Maybe you've even made specific goals to help you achieve such a life. Now you just want to discover the missing key to unlock the door to God's blessing for your life.

Or perhaps you've almost lost hope. You feel like the Christian life is too good to be true; you can never attain it. Don't give up! In this book you'll find direction, encouragement and hope.

If you seriously follow the biblical principles outlined in this book, I'm convinced you will be spiritually renewed by the Lord Jesus Christ long before you turn the last page. God longs and desires to radically transform every area of your life. And if you let Him, He will!

The steps to radical renewal outlined in this book revolutionized my own life. But I almost threw in the towel before finally learning all of them in a rather piecemeal fashion. I learned one principle at age seventeen. Another at age twenty. At twenty-five another vital understanding.

Obviously, the Lord has kept me growing through the years. He's blessed my life and ministry. But before I experienced any of that blessing, certain necessary and achievable steps were required. I pass them on to you in the hope that you may avoid the years of frustration I experienced.

This book is packed with truth from God's Word. Read it with a Bible close at hand—as though you and I were talking all this over together—until these marvellous realities are yours. Until they are so second nature that you're ready to present them to others.

This book isn't theory. It shows you specific, practical steps that work. Essential steps so you can enter into God's best for your life. While you're reading this book, you can embark on a new way of life with your heavenly Father. You can stop saying and thinking and doing things that keep you feeling defeated, depressed, guilty, inadequate, lethargic, fruitless and frustrated. You can become vibrant, victorious, cheerful, and dynamic—honouring and exalting God in thought, word and deed.

For several years after I met Christ, I could be quite moody, worried, fearful and anxious. Sometimes loud and angry, other times morose and despondent. It seemed I worked and worked, but saw little or no fruit.

When I finally took all the steps to radical renewal, the Lord changed me into a joyful and fruitful servant of His. Not that I don't grieve the Holy Spirit and fail to display His fruit at times, but the difference in my life has been dramatic. I love Him for it beyond expression.

Throughout history thousands have lived positive, free, Spirit-filled, God-honouring, pure and holy lives. One way or another, they all walked the same path outlined in this book. Radical renewal can be our experience, too, by God's grace.

HOW TO USE THIS BOOK

Let's take just a moment to talk about how to use this book. I recommend that you read this book once straight through as quickly as possible. You'll notice that part one is mostly narrative, while part two is more practical. But don't stop to put the steps I recommend into practice yet.

After a quick initial reading, start over and read this book again more slowly. This time have a Bible, notebook and pen on hand. Make notes and take each step in the order recommended. Underline or highlight any statements or sections in the book that seem especially significant to you.

Review this book again in a few weeks. Especially note the statements and sections you highlighted or underlined the second time through. Use a different coloured pen to make additional notes. Ask God to use the biblical principles outlined in this book to truly renew you.

Then if *Radical Renewal* is a help to you, why not recommend it to a friend? You may even want to suggest using this book as the basis for a two- or three-month series in your home Bible study, fellowship group, or Sunday school class.

Finally, write to me, please! It would be great to hear how the Lord is using the principles in this book to change you. The address is 36 Sycamore Road, Amersham, Buckinghamshire HP6 5DR. I look forward to corresponding with you.

Are you ready, then? Ready for a lifelong adventure? Ready to experience God's blessing and favour on your life? That is His marvellous design and desire for you!

PART ONE

———

'Happiness is neither within us only, or without:
it is our union with God.'
—Pascal

CHAPTER 1

IS EVERYBODY HAPPY?

*Before discussing the principles of radical
renewal in detail, let me tell you a few stories
that are on my heart....*

Do you like being a Christian?

Sure, you've said 'yes' to Jesus Christ for your salvation. But are you saying 'yes!' to everything He has in store for you? Or have you tried and wound up feeling more frustrated than fulfilled?

There are a surprising number of dissatisfied Christians in our churches today. They don't necessarily look so unhappy on the outside, when you see them in the congregation on Sunday morning. In fact, they're often very busy people, serving on church committees and teaching Sunday school classes. But when you have an opportunity to explore behind the new clothes and plastic smiles, you discover that many people really don't enjoy being Christians.

Crest View is a strong missions-minded church, supporting a broad range of missionary efforts on four continents. Which is where I enter the picture. The church started supporting my wife and me in the late sixties when we were still serving as missionaries in Mexico City. Despite the fact that I'd only visited a couple of times in the past twenty years, they stayed with us as we expanded our evangelistic ministry throughout Latin America and into Europe and other parts of the world. To say the least, I felt more than a little obligated (despite a rather tight schedule) when Crest View's new pastor invited me to speak on the opening Sunday of their annual missions conference.

The last time I was back there, Crest View had a congregation of about 350 people and its new sanctuary was nearly full on a good Sunday. Now Sunday morning attendance was up to 800, with two packed morning services, plus a strong evening service. This seemed like a thriving congregation— healthy, growing, eager to continue reaching out.

I looked forward to the opportunity to reestablish ties with Crest View, spend time with the new pastor, speak at the local seminary, and even squeeze in a quick interview with a local newspaper reporter on the side.

I didn't expect to find burned out ministers, feuding members, and long-established families coming apart.

I flew to the city Saturday afternoon. On Sunday morning, I arrived twenty minutes before the first service. I was impressed with how smoothly the church functioned. The choir director was arranging his music on the platform. The ushers were already at their posts, greeting early arrivals. At precisely 8:45, the pastors and I started our prayer meeting in a small room behind the platform. And at 9:00 sharp, the four of us stepped onto the platform.

As is my habit, I began studying the faces in the congregation during the opening minutes of the worship service. Bill Donaldson, who had picked me up at the airport, was seated in the front row with his wife. A group of singles were scattered on the left-hand side pews. A cluster of teens were joking and whispering in the back of the balcony. I recognized several families I'd met during my last visit, but tried in vain to remember any of their names. I've got to try to get back here more often, I thought.

These people looked so alive. They were dressed well. If looks reflected the inner heart of this congregation, it was vibrant and healthy. For a moment, I wished I'd chosen a more mission-oriented message. But I checked myself; looks were often deceiving. Everything looked fine on the outside, but what did God see on the inside?

After Pastor Michaelson introduced me, I moved quickly to the pulpit and preached from my heart. My text was John 13, and it was only remotely related to the theme of missions. Normally I'd select a passage like John 14:12-15, where Jesus talks about our doing greater things than the Son, and preach about gaining a vision for world evangelism. But the Lord seemed to say, 'What use is it to talk about the "greater works" Jesus Christ wants to do through us if we've stifled His work in our own heart?' Thus, my decision to preach about confession and cleansing as pictured by Jesus washing the disciples' feet. I would make it work as a missions message by throwing in a few illustrations from my experiences overseas, and by inviting the congregation back for my second message that night.

The congregation seemed very attentive. Several nodded their heads, obviously responding positively to my words. But I could tell there were a few who were uncomfortable with my message. What hidden nerves were my words touching?

During the next service I recognized several more families, including a prominent businessman, Paul Nichols, who was going through the throes of bankruptcy during my last visit. A series of business reversals created a domino effect on his old financial empire. But I'd heard that he was repaying all his debts and had a thriving new business that employed several Crest View members. I was curious to find out more.

By the end of the second service, I felt genuinely welcomed at Crest View and could hardly wait to preach again that night. The congregation in both services had been especially warm and responsive.

As I walked toward the front door with the pastor, an usher handed me a note addressed to 'Mr. Palau.' I read it quickly: 'Luis, you talked this morning about enjoying a happy and holy life. What you said about guilt and cleansing was okay. I've done all that. But how come I'm still not happy?' The note was signed, 'A Sunday School Teacher.' I put it in my pocket and decided to try to answer the question during my message that evening.

At the front door, Paul Nichols shook my hand and asked if I would join them for dinner at their home before the service that night.

I spent the afternoon over at Pastor Michaelson's home. Dinner was fine and his children were pleasant, but his wife seemed uptight. I sensed something was on the pastor's mind. I decided to probe while we relaxed in his backyard.

'How long have you been at Crest View now?' I asked.

'It must be almost eighteen months. Yes, eighteen months next Sunday in fact.'

'How do you like it here?' He told me about how he felt called of God to accept this pastorate, and commented that 'the Lord has been good to us here'. He cited growing attendance and the new building programme as examples.

'How does your wife like it here?' Pastor Michaelson looked away for a moment. Then these words spewed out. 'Luis, every pastor I know is frustrated, unfulfilled and ready to move on. The only person more frustrated is his wife. That's true of Joanie and me.'

Pastor Michaelson went on to tell me that the average pastor in his denomination changed pastorates once every twenty months. 'The hardest question I wrestle with is, Why should I stay?'

Later that afternoon, Pastor Michaelson drove me over to the Nichols'. On the way, we talked further about his frustrations and his wife's persistent desire to move on to something 'bigger and better'. Mostly, I listened, but I couldn't help mentally noting that Crest View is considered a big, successful church by most pastors. Did this mean the end of the line for this pastor? Was he thinking of moving into another vocation?

'Joanie's desperate, Luis. She can't stand this place. I've never seen her so distant, so determined to get her own way.

And who am I to stop her? I've about had it myself. What's the point of living a frustrating life of sacrifice without meaning?'

There was so much I wanted to say, principles from God's Word that have revolutionized my life and ministry. But to go into them in depth could take a couple of hours, and we had reached our destination.

The Nichols' home seemed more modest than I would have expected. Paul and his wife Nancy had lived in quite an estate before. As we talked, I learned that they actually had owned several expensive homes and a resort beach house before their financial troubles began.

Paul had been president of a bank, and had large oil and real estate investments to top it off. Socially, the Nichols had been invited to all the key social and political events. Then the economy in their state took a nosedive and their financial empire began falling piece by piece, like so many dominoes.

Within two years the Nichols were bankrupt, through no wrongdoing of their own. They gave up their jet, sold their cars, and finally put their homes on the market in an attempt to pay back their debts. During this period, Paul and Nancy's marriage and Christian faith were tested to the limit. What had been theory became reality. They clung to the Lord and believed that somehow, unexplainable to them, He was still in control of their lives.

To meet the Nichols today, you'd never guess they've been through a trauma that most couples wouldn't survive. Their marriage seems vibrant and their outlook is others-focused, not self-centered. While Paul seemed to be thriving spiritually, he was concerned about a fellow Crest View member, Tony, who was also an employee in Paul's company.

Apparently Tony, a trusted middle manager, had improperly used the company's personnel, time and assets to develop a small business on the side. He thought he could keep his little venture quiet behind Paul's back. When Paul learned about the scheme, he confronted him with the facts but Tony lied to Paul. Several employees admitted, however, that they were working on the side for Tony during company time. Tony finally admitted he'd made a 'mistake', but Paul felt he wasn't truly repentant. 'How do I handle a situation like this?' he asked.

We discussed the principles from Matthew and other passages about how to deal with someone who has sinned, and if that doesn't work, to take witnesses to verify the information, and finally, if necessary, to take the matter to the church. Paul agreed that the matter needed to be dealt with biblically. 'My primary concern is that Tony claims to be a Christian, but he hasn't allowed God to deal with some basic areas in his life.'

During the evening service, I challenged the congregation to dedicate themselves to God. 'Whether God is calling you to missionary service isn't my question tonight. I'll leave that for others later this week. But the issue is, Have you surrendered your rights to God? Have you given Him the title deed to your life? Are you willing to choose His will, whatever it may be?'

I was surrounded by people after the service. I hadn't noticed Marlene during the service, but recognized her immediately when she walked up. My wife Pat and I had known Marlene and Nate before they were married sixteen years ago.

Marlene and Nate looked like a great couple on their way to a happy, successful life when I saw them last. Nate was a commercial artist; Marlene was active as a women's Bible study leader. They had three kids and apparently a solid home. Then Nate joined a local popular singing group. In that group was a woman, also married, who was a charming and fun-loving person. Soon thereafter Nate announced that he was bored and abruptly left Marlene.

Pat had corresponded with Marlene several times since then, helping her deal with the trauma of divorce and the dozens of questions that follow. So I had some idea what was behind Marlene's initial 'thank you'. Then she paused a moment, wiped away a tear, and said, 'It's okay now. Tell Pat that God's holding on to me, and I know He won't let me go.'

Inside I cried for Marlene. We all thought Nate was a

committed Christian. What had gone wrong? Yet I knew Nate's turning his back on God and leaving Marlene was anything but a unique case. In fact, in a church this size, there were bound to be others.

There wasn't time to dwell on Marlene's pain as other people wanted to talk to me. Rick was a young man who introduced himself by saying he was active in a chemical dependency support group that met at another church nearby on Monday nights. When I asked him about the group, he said he felt the group gave him the strength to stay off cocaine. He had been an active drug abuser before joining the group four years ago.

Then Rick got to the point. 'Both this morning and tonight you talked a lot about Jesus' power to change people's lives. You talked about the need to get into God's Word. You talked about what the Lord could do through us once He's changed us from the inside out. But you almost made it sound like it could happen overnight.' His voice was filled with tension as he continued, 'It doesn't work that way.'

With that, Rick abruptly turned around and walked off before I could reply. Immediately, another young man stepped up and asked if he could talk with me privately. After I greeted a few others, we walked together over to an empty corner of the auditorium. 'My name is Tony,' he said. I immediately wondered if this was the same guy Paul Nichols had told me about after dinner. It was.

Tony gave me his version of the story: 'I was bending the rules at work a bit and the boss isn't taking it very lightly.'

I asked a few questions, then went to the heart of the matter. 'In each of our lives, often at a crisis point, we must come to the place where we consciously choose God's will over and against our own will. Where we acknowledge God as God of every area of our lives. Where we offer ourselves— body, soul and spirit—to the Lord. Where we hold nothing back. I wonder if God is using this crisis to give you an opportunity to make that decision?'

Tony and I talked until they finally dimmed the lights in

the sanctuary. I felt convinced that he was beginning to see his basic dishonesty and need to dedicate himself wholeheartedly to God. So I invited Tony to join me across the street at the restaurant adjacent to my motel.

We talked for nearly an hour and a half. Tony finally broke down and quietly wept about his deception at work. But within a couple of minutes his faced hardened and he cynically dismissed the idea of dedicating himself to God. He was so close. But he'd counted the cost and decided that he had to give up too much of his own desires in order to follow Christ. I was heartbroken over Tony's decision, but as we parted, he half promised to stay in contact.

On Monday morning, I spoke at a special chapel service at the seminary. Knowing this would be my only opportunity to talk with these students, I wondered, How do I say everything I want to say in forty-five minutes? There wasn't time to exegete a number of New Testament passages at length. So I decided to challenge them to do the work themselves.

'If you carefully read through the New Testament, you'll discover that one of its primary themes is God's desire to indwell us and fill us, and from that overflow to do good works through us. Luke frequently speaks of the filling of the Spirit. Paul mentions that once, but talks again and again about the fact that "Christ lives in me" or "Christ is in you". Study it for yourself and think through the implications. If this can get from your head to your heart, it could totally revolutionize your Christian experience.'

After the chapel service, several seminarians crowded around the front to talk with me. One young man shared his dream of becoming an evangelist. I asked for his address so we could keep in touch; I have a burden for fanning into flame the burden such young men have for evangelism.

Another young seminarian expressed frustration over his lack of evangelistic fervour and boldness. 'You talked about gaining a passion for the lost, but I feel a real credibility problem. First, I just can't get all worked up about the lost. How do we know it isn't going to work out okay for most of them in the end, anyway? And second, who am I to try to tell others what a difference the Lord can make in their lives when I can't see that much of a difference in my own life?'

When I heard those words, I realized this young man was only expressing what many thought. Yet this was a future pastor for a church like Crest View. Was he going to wind up bitter and frustrated like Pastor Michaelson?

Really, others at Crest View were saying the same thing, in their own ways. They probably wanted to see God use them, but they knew they were hypocrites. They were so tied up in their own failings that they couldn't possibly enjoy their faith, much less reach out to others.

Back at the motel, I was met by Mark Jensen, religious reporter for a daily newspaper. He seemed very open and supportive of what I was doing, and knowledgeable about my team's recent evangelistic campaigns in Eastern Europe and Asia.

During the next hour, I probably interviewed Mark almost as much as he interviewed me. I discovered that he was a former pastor. Cautiously I asked why he stepped out of the ministry and into secular employment.

It turned out that Mark hadn't committed any great sin; he just couldn't take the frustrations of the pastorate anymore. 'To be honest, Luis, I felt that most of what I did as a pastor was meaningless,' Mark said. 'I'm still a committed Christian. I plan on being faithful to the end. But the ministry wasn't what I thought it was going to be. Journalism is much more satisfying. I get to cover real issues and see real results from my work almost every day.'

Once again, I thought back to my conversations with Pastor Michaelson and wondered if things would turn out any different for him.

Prior to my flight back home, I had a dinner engagement with Bill and Joyce Donaldson. Their dining room was so large and so well decorated that, with the slightly dimmed lighting, I almost forgot we weren't at a restaurant. Bill asked lots of questions about my ministry and what I thought about various world events as they related to missions.

Gradually, I learned that they both had graduated from one of the best private universities. Bill had inherited a large sum of money and his profession was paying off well. They were active at Crest View, especially with the church's missions committee. 'What sparked your interest in missions?' I asked.

'Well, Joyce and I both trusted Christ during our university days. We were quite active in one of the Christian student groups on campus, and at one point seriously considered going to the mission field ourselves.'

'What changed your minds?'

'Nothing that I can think of,' said Joyce. 'We were anxious to get married, then Bill landed a good job at the company. We've been active at Crest View ever since. God has been good to us here. With the kids and everything, it would be hard to even think of leaving now.'

'Besides,' added Bill, 'the glamour isn't there anymore. Missions is a tough row to hoe. It's a lot of sacrifice, but very little thanks. If it wasn't for all the work we do on the missions committee, I doubt the average person at Crest View could tell you who half our missionaries are. We find it a struggle just to get people to pray for them once in a while.

'And the missionaries certainly don't get any standing ovation when they come back on furlough. We try to make them feel at home, but some can't wait to get back on the field after a few months. And then when they retire, what? Most haven't got a penny in the bank.'

On my flight back to Portland that evening, I felt a heavy burden. Except for the Nichols, and maybe the Donaldsons, it seemed like most of the Christians I had met during the last couple of days were missing the whole point of the Christian life.

I wondered what was in store for the Michaelsons, Rick, Tony, Mark and the seminary students with whom I'd talked. As I had listened to their stories, I could relate to many of them. Not to the details, of course, but to the underlying desire to please God, the distractions, the frustrations, and the overwhelming temptation to give up. I'd had that same experience.

Perhaps you can relate to some of this, too. Have you ever felt fruitless? Frustrated? Unfulfilled? Almost ready to call it quits?

This book is for anyone who feels like there has to be more to the life Jesus Christ offers than what you've experienced so far. Well, there is! Much more! But, as you'll discover in the next chapter, I almost threw in the towel before proving it for myself.

CHAPTER 2

WHY I ALMOST GAVE UP

*The steps to radical renewal revolutionized my
life, but I almost gave up before finally learning
all of them in a rather piecemeal fashion....*

If you would like an example of a totally dedicated Christian,
there's probably no better example than me as a young man.
That isn't meant as a statement of pride, because I was not
living the Christian life as God intended it. Rather, I was the
epitome of human effort, trying to do what is impossible to
do in our flesh—live a life pleasing to God.

As you'll soon see, I was doing all of the right outward
things, but I was headed for defeat just as surely as Tony or
Pastor Michaelson or that anonymous Sunday school teacher
at Crest View Church.

It all started on a cold night in the mountains of southern
Argentina. A light rain had started spattering against the roof
of an army tent that housed ten boys. Some fifty or sixty of us
boys were spending two weeks at an outdoor camp organized
by one of my teachers, Charles Cohen. We were totally cut
off from the outside world. There were no radios or news-
papers, so we couldn't learn the football scores. Instead, we
were saturated with the Bible and gospel songs.

Each night, the counsellor in each tent took one of the boys
for a walk and gave him the opportunity to say yes or no to
Jesus Christ's claims upon his life. All the other boys had had
their chance, so I knew tonight was my turn. I wished that I

could run and hide from it, because I was embarrassed that I had not received Christ yet.

My counsellor, Frank Chandler, tried to rouse me from sleep. Actually, I was only pretending to sleep. 'Come on, Luis, get up!' Frank ordered. I kept my eyes shut and didn't move. He shook me, then shined his flashlight in my eyes. He knew I couldn't be that unconscious, so he tipped over my cot and dumped me on the floor. I slipped on my canvas-topped shoes and put on a jacket. We heard thunder in the distance and knew a real rainstorm was coming. Frank was in a hurry. I wasn't. Little did I know that this was going to be the best night of camp.

Frank walked me to a fallen log, where we sat and talked. There were no preliminaries. 'Luis,' he asked, 'are you a Christian or not?'

'I don't think so,' I said.

'Well, it's not a matter of whether you think so or not. Are you or aren't you?'

'No, I'm not.'

Like many others in the camp, I grew up attending Sunday school and church. I knew many songs and choruses and stories. If someone asked me, I could stand up and quote a few verses. I could even say a prayer if you asked me. But I felt a tremendous burden of guilt. My foul mouth and impure sexual thoughts made me afraid of God's judgement.

Frank pulled out his flashlight and opened his New Testament. 'If you died tonight, would you go to heaven or to hell?'

I sat quietly for a moment, somewhat taken aback, and then said, 'I'd go to hell.'

'Is that where you want to go?'

'No.'

'Then why are you going there?'

I shrugged my shoulders. 'I don't know.'

Chandler turned in his Bible and read Romans 10:9-10—'If you confess with your lips, Luis, that Jesus is Lord and believe in your heart, Luis, that God raised Him from the dead, you, Luis, will be saved. For man believes with his heart and so is justified, and he confesses with his lips and so is saved.'

He looked at me. 'Luis, do you believe in your heart that God raised Jesus from the dead?'

'Yes, I do,' I said.

'Then what do you have to do next to be saved?'

I hesitated. The rain started coming down harder. Chandler had me read Romans 10:9 once more—'If you confess with your lips that Jesus is Lord...you will be saved.'

'Luis, are you ready to confess Him as your Lord right now?'

'Yes.'

'All right, let's pray.' Chandler put his arm around me and right there, sitting in the rain, I made my decision. 'Lord Jesus, I believe You were raised from the dead,' I prayed. 'I confess You with my lips. Give me eternal life. I want to be Yours. Save me from hell. Amen.'

When we finished praying, I was crying. I gave Chandler a big hug and we ran back to the tent. I crawled under my blanket with my flashlight and wrote in my Bible, 'On February 12, 1947, I received Jesus Christ as my Saviour.'

I was only twelve years old, but I knew I was born again. I was saved! I was a member of the family of God. I had eternal life because Christ said, 'I give them eternal life, and they shall never perish; no one can snatch them out of my hand' (John 10:28). I was so excited that I could hardly sleep. After all, this is the most important decision anyone can ever make.

That initial excitement about my new life in Christ lasted for some months. I told all my friends about it, and began carrying my Bible with me a lot. I became more active than ever in Bible club, and the Anglican church services we were required to attend at the British boarding school I attended took on a whole new meaning to me. I was even baptized and confirmed. I sang in the choir, until my terrible voice got me thrown out, and I began to study my Bible every day. I corresponded often with Frank Chandler. And I became a

much better student, especially in Charles Cohen's Acts of the
Apostles class.

There's not a more open and teachable mind than that of a
child still excited over his conversion. I could visualize the
cities and movements of the early church in Acts, because it
was so clearly taught. Years later, when I studied the same
course at the graduate level, I found that I already knew most
of it from that semester as a twelve-year-old.

No one has ever adequately explained the loss of that first
excitement and love for Christ. When I lost it, it was as if
someone had pulled my plug and the lights went out. Perhaps
I let a cynical attitude get in the way. Perhaps I ignored my
mother's counsel to stay away from worldly influences, like
listening to football matches on Sunday and going to movies.
Or perhaps I was succumbing to the pressures of my fellow
students.

All I know is that one day, coming home from Bible club, I
carelessly left my Bible on a bus and was unable to get it back.
With that loss went my daily Bible reading, my attendance at
Bible club, my excitement over Bible class, and almost everything that went along with my commitment to Jesus Christ. I
still loved and believed and respected the Gospel, but I didn't
let it interfere with my life.

This attitude lasted four long years. I've since tried to
determine just what went wrong. Essentially, I had no idea
about how to live a victorious life. I had been taught the basics
well, but I was into a spirituality based on performance.
Praying, reading, studying and going to church can wear thin
fast, if that's all there is to a person's faith. I don't recall
picking up any instruction on how to enjoy Christ, how to
praise and worship Him, how to walk with Him and be happy
in Him. I found myself bored with an endless repetition of the
routine.

Though I take full responsibility, three things contributed
to my straying into the world. First, my father had not left a
will when he died unexpectedly at age thirty-five. I was just
ten at the time, much too young to have any say about the

family business. Several of my relatives took over the business, and within three years ruined it, leaving us destitute. I was not equipped to forgive them, and the rage I felt as a young man was intense.

Second, there was the lure of the world and non-Christian friends. I was attracted to a life of parties and football games and listening to the radio—hardly bad things in themselves, but indicative of my loss of interest in spiritual things.

My mother did everything she could to see that I continued in private school. Since I was part Scottish, the English Aid society gave me a partial subsidy on my tuition. But I was forced to live with my grandparents and commute to school to save money. It was humiliating, and it also put me in a position to be less disciplined during my free time. Fortunately, even my non-Christian friends from my new neighbourhood were pretty straight, or I could have gotten into really big trouble. Even though the family was nearly bankrupt, and the business had virtually folded, I told my friends that it was thriving and just waiting for me to come back and run it. I bragged about how I was going to be rich and powerful, a self-made businessman. Only I was lying. By the time I was sixteen, I secretly blamed God for most of our troubles. I had come full circle from my first love of Him to where I thought He had let us down.

The third factor was when my mother told me I could not continue in boarding school. I had dreamed of qualifying for the graduate course at Cambridge University, but I fell one year short, finishing with the equivalent of a junior college degree.

I felt I had been the victim of a cruel joke. Eight long, double years of schooling in the British boarding schools had left me with an intermediate degree, no money, and, as far as I could tell, no future. I still feared God, but I questioned Him daily. I was glad that I had not served Him more. I felt He owed me better than what I was getting, so why should I live for Him? Deep down, though, I knew I was wrong and that I should return to Him.

I never made fun of the church, as some of my friends and relatives did. But I went sparingly, and then only to please my grandmother. I entered late and left early, doing my best to appear uninterested. It wasn't difficult. I joined the local university club and bought myself a pipe. I studied a Dale Carnegie book and learned 'how to win friends and influence people', by acting interested in any small detail about the other person's life. I was a fast-talking, smooth-working phony. Inside I hated myself. My friends, although non-Christians, were really super kids; by most standards, they were straight. Besides, the fear of the Lord kept me from going off the deep end into any gross sin.

The turning point came just before Carnival Week in February. It's a week of total abandonment before Lent, followed by forty days of confession and penance. So during the carnival, anything went. Any business not crucial to the festivities was closed for the whole week.

I had grown tired of the sophisticated little parties and games the university club offered. Doing something more bizarre sounded like an exciting alternative. So my friends and I made big plans for celebrating Carnival Week.

The more I thought about it, however, the more ominous it became. Somehow I felt that if I went to Carnival Week, temptation would overwhelm me and I would be engulfed in sin. I knew my mother and other relatives prayed daily that I would walk with the Lord. The more I thought about it the more panicky I became. If I participated in the carnival, I felt I could sever my relationship with the Lord. While in my head I knew that nothing could separate me from the love of Christ, in my heart I feared God might not forgive this out-and-out mockery of everything I had been taught.

I'm sure the Holy Spirit was convicting me. Toying with the world was one thing, but abandoning self-respect and flaunting God's law was something else. There was no purpose in my life, nothing to look forward to except more of the same empty 'fun'. If I went to Carnival Week, I was convinced I would have gone beyond that point of no return. I had to get out of it. My grandparents were gone that weekend, and the house was empty. The next day my friends would come by to pick me up for the festivities. I didn't have the strength to simply tell them I wasn't going. I had to have a reason. Falling to my knees by my bed, I pleaded with God: 'Get me out of this and I will give up everything that's of the world. I will serve You and give my whole life to You. Just get me out of this!'

I had no idea how God would get me out of my dilemma without my having to lie. I didn't want to do that. To prove that I meant business, I pulled my grandmother's Bible from a drawer and put it on the table beside the bed.

The next morning I awoke, slowly sat up, swung my legs over the side of the bed onto the floor, and sat there a moment. I yawned. My mouth felt strange. I touched it. I felt no pain, but it was bloated.

I stumbled to the mirror. My mouth was so swollen it looked as if I'd spent several hours at the dentist. Staring at my reflection, I worked up a crooked smile. 'God has answered my prayer,' I said aloud.

I called up one of my friends. 'I can't go to the dance tonight, and I won't be going to the carnival at all this week.'

'Come on Luis. Everything has been planned.'

'No. I have a good reason, and I will not go.'

'You must be crazy! I'll be right over.'

A few minutes later he showed up with three or four of the others. They insisted that the swelling would go down and that I should change my mind. But by then I had a good head of steam going, and I resisted until they left. I should have told my friends that, because of my faith in the Lord Jesus, I was afraid of the sin I might get involved in at the carnival. That's what I would tell them today. But I was so spiritually bankrupt that it took that fat lip to deliver me.

Knowing how good the Gospel is, I am ashamed that I was so cowardly. But at least I had made my decision, taken my stand, and broken with the world. I went back into the house, and to symbolize my new resolve, I snapped my pipe in two, tore up my university club membership card, and threw away all my football and car-racing magazines and many record albums.

The next day I went to church morning and night. The rest of the town, it seemed, was frolicking in sin. But I had escaped. Everything seemed different. Life perked up and had meaning again. I even bought a new Bible to demonstrate my fresh dedication to walk with God. Looking back, I'm so thankful for the promise of Philippians 1:6—'And I am sure that God who began the good work within you will keep right on helping you grow in his grace until his task within you is finally finished on that day when Jesus Christ returns' (TLB). Slowly I was seeing that, although I might fail God many times in my life, He would never fail me. I was learning, step by step, what it meant to live a godly, joyful, fruitful life. The most crucial step, however, was still ahead. Almost eight years ahead, to be exact.

Trying Too Hard

After dedicating my life to Christ, some of my teenage friends and I started all night prayer meetings, every Friday night. We wanted to prove that we really meant business. We'd take coffee and cookies to stay awake during the early morning hours. We confessed our sins, we laid hands on each other, we read promises, we prayed for the lost, we prayed for the church. Mostly, we prayed about temptations we didn't know how to handle.

Whenever a great preacher came to our church, we tried to get an interview with him. Our questions were always the same. 'How can we get victory over temptation? How can we live holy lives? What do we have to do?'

Usually the visiting preacher would ask, 'Are you reading the Bible?'

'Yes, we get up at 5:00 every morning before going to school or work. We read several chapters every day.'

'Great! But are you testifying for Jesus?'

'Yes. We hand out tracts, teach children's classes, and even hold street meetings.'

'That's terrific! But are you praying?' the preacher would ask. So we'd tell him all about our all-night prayer meetings. Our frustration must have been obvious. 'What else do we need to do?' we'd ask.

'Well, pray some more, witness some more, read the Bible some more.' So we did. And we just about killed ourselves, we were so eager to be holy.

Others would urge us from the pulpit to rededicate our lives to Jesus Christ. So we went forward. But I still had many of the same feelings of frustration and inadequacy. 'Maybe there's some area of my life I still haven't dedicated to the Lord.' So I went to the 'altar', and re-rededicated my life. A year later I super re-rededicated my life! But something still wasn't working.

Some of my friends started dropping out of our all-night prayer meetings. Others stopped going to church altogether. Some slipped out quietly, others ended up in blatant sin. But they all had a sense of despair. 'We've read the Bible like mad. We've prayed all night. We've witnessed for Christ, but we still can't say no to certain temptations. Either the Gospel doesn't work,' they concluded, 'or I'm such a sinner that even God can't keep me from having dirty thoughts, or whatever.'

One friend cynically made fun of the verses that speak of Christian victory. When I ran across a good book on the subject, my friend said, 'Well, I'd like to see how victorious that author would be if he were under a broken-down car, with oil dripping all over him.' I couldn't argue with that and fell into the same type of cynicism, mostly because I couldn't find victory myself. I figured he must be right; true victory wasn't possible.

I hung in there. Barely. I loved the Word, and studied it diligently, but I never got the point of what it means to walk in the Spirit without being legalistic. I longed to be free of the self-effort of the flesh. My times of study and prayer and work became a cycle of grim determination to keep on keeping on. I knew the power was to come from the Spirit, but for some reason I didn't experience it. I continued to search desperately, when I should have long since found it.

I was on the verge of giving up, not because I saw any lack in God, but because I was weary of fighting and struggling and seeking on my own to persevere through sheer dedication. I was exhausted, and exhaustion can breed cynicism.

When am I ever going to catch on? I wondered. Will I give up now, after all I've been through? I knew the other side of life was hopeless. But there is a monumental emptiness when you know you're looking in the right place and still not finding the answer. I wanted to please and love and serve God. I wanted people to be saved. I would sing, 'Oh, Jesus, I have promised to serve Thee to the end,' and I would think, Even if it kills me.

One day I was invited to hear Jim Savage speak about the possibility of Billy Graham coming to Argentina. What impressed me most—besides the size of the crowd (just over a thousand, as big as I'd ever seen for anything evangelical in our community)—was a brief film of Dr. Graham speaking to Christian leaders in India.

The film showed an unbelievable crowd of tens of thousands, but the dramatic effect the camera left was of Billy Graham talking directly to us. He was preaching from Ephesians 5:18—'Do not get drunk on wine, which leads to debauchery. Instead, be filled with the Spirit.' It was as if the crowd in India didn't exist. He was looking right at me and shouting, 'Are you filled with the Spirit? Are you filled with the Spirit? Are you filled with the Spirit?'

I knew that was my problem—I wasn't filled with the Spirit. That was the reason for my up-and-down Christianity. That's why I had zeal and commitment, but little fruit or victory. When would it end? When would I find the answer?

I found it thanks to a British preacher after several frustrating months of graduate work in the United States.

I came to the States through the patient prodding of a prominent pastor named Ray Stedman. The first two months,

I lived in his home. I was argumentative and wanted to discuss theology and doctrine for hours. I had come to learn, but maybe I wasn't yet ready to admit that I didn't have all the answers. Ray and Elaine and their four daughters were so patient and understanding that their harmony pervaded the place, in spite of the fiery Latin who had invaded their home. Ray's humour kept everyone happy, and we all became fast friends.

Two months with the Stedmans wasn't enough time to learn the American culture—how to chat and eat and behave the way the natives do—but it was all I had before going north to Multnomah School of the Bible in Portland, Oregon. Multnomah is a very demanding school, and I found the first semester particularly rough.

What made it particularly frustrating was that our Spiritual Life class professor, Dr. George Kehoe, began every class period by quoting Galatians 2:20—'I have been crucified with Christ and I no longer live, but Christ lives in me. The life I live in the body, I live by faith in the Son of God, who loved me and gave himself for me.'

I was still struggling to find more fruit in my personal spiritual life. I was frustrated in not being able to live out the life-style I saw in men like Ray Stedman and several others at Peninsula Bible Church. Their lives exhibited a joy and freedom that I found attractive. But the more I sought it, the more elusive it became.

My spiritual journey seemed like a climb up a tall cliff. I clawed every inch of the way uphill only to slip and slide back down. Although I had experienced many times of blessing and victory, for the most part I felt the struggle was impossible. I couldn't go on that way, especially when no one else knew about it. It was my secret, private death. There was a limit to how long I could hold on to the side of this cliff. If I didn't get help soon, I was going to let go altogether.

I felt like a sincere hypocrite. People laugh when I say that, but I truly was, and it wasn't funny. Some hypocrites know they are hypocrites and want to be that way. They want to have two lives: one to show off at church and one to live in private. I simply wanted to be the person people thought I was.

If I were to describe myself in those days, I would have to say I was envious, jealous, too preoccupied and self-centered, and ambitious to a wrong degree. I was smug about other speakers, silently rating their illustrations or delivery against my own. That left me feeling mean and ugly and petty. No amount of wrestling with myself would rid me of those sins. And yet I tried. I felt despicable; I hated the idea that I was a hypocrite.

Maybe that's why I didn't like the constant reminder of Galatians 2:20. I was getting so annoyed at Dr. Kehoe's quoting that verse every day that I had to ask myself why. It can't be a Bible verse that gets you so upset, I told myself. It must be you. Yet rather than let that verse penetrate my pride, I decided instead that the verse was self-contradictory, hard to understand, and confusing, especially in English.

Shortly before Christmas break, Major Ian Thomas spoke at our chapel service. I had taken to sitting in the back of the auditorium during daily chapel, where we usually got another dose of exposition or missionary stories. I dared the speaker to make me pay attention. If he was good, I'd honour him by listening. Otherwise I would daydream or peek at my class notes.

Major Thomas was founder and general director of the Torchbearers in England, the group that runs the Capernwray Hall Bible School. His British accent and staccato delivery caught my attention, but what really intrigued me was the way he pointed at us with a finger that had been partially amputated. While his speaking style hooked me, his short message spoke to me. Ian Thomas talked about Moses, and how it took this great man forty years in the wilderness to learn that he was nothing. Then one day, Moses was confronted with a burning bush. Thomas said that the burning bush in the desert was likely a dry bunch of ugly little sticks that had hardly developed, yet Moses had to take off his shoes. Why was it holy ground? Because God was in the bush!

Here was Major Thomas' point. God was telling Moses, 'I don't need a pretty bush or an educated bush or an eloquent bush. Any old bush will do, as long as I am in the bush. If I am going to use you, I am going to use you. It will not be you doing something for Me, but Me doing something through you.'

It suddenly hit me that I was that kind of bush: the worthless, useless bunch of dried-up sticks. I could do nothing for God. All my reading and studying and asking questions and trying to model myself after others was worthless. Everything in my ministry was worthless, unless God was in the bush. Only He could make something happen. Only He could make it work.

Thomas told of many Christian workers who failed at first because they thought they had something to offer God. He himself had once imagined that because he was an aggressive, winsome, evangelistic sort, God would use him. But God didn't use him until he came to the end of himself. That's exactly my situation, I thought. I am at the end of myself.

Thomas closed his message by reading Galatians 2:20. And then it all came together for me. 'I have been crucified with Christ and I no longer live, but Christ lives in me.' My biggest spiritual struggle was finally over! I would let God be God and let Luis Palau be dependent upon Him.

You can't imagine the complete release I felt, as a result of that little chapel talk. I ran back to my room in tears and fell to my knees next to my bunk. I prayed in my native Spanish, 'Lord, now I understand! The whole thing is "not I, but Christ in me". It's not what I'm going to do for You but rather what You're going to do through me.'

I stayed on my knees until lunchtime, an hour and a half later, to stay in communion with the Lord. I realized that the reason I hated myself inside was because I wrongly loved myself outside. I asked God's forgiveness for my pride. Oh, I was really something, I had thought, but God was not active in the bush. I hadn't given Him the chance.

Well, God still had a lot of burning to do, but God was finally in control of this bush. He wanted me to be grateful for all the small hinges He had put in my life, but He didn't want me to place my confidence in those opportunities to make me a better minister or preacher. He wanted me to depend not on myself or my breaks, but on Christ alone—the indwelling, resurrected, almighty Lord Jesus.

I was thrilled to finally realize that we have everything we need when we have Jesus Christ literally living in us. Our inner resource is God Himself, because of our union with Jesus Christ (see Colossians 2:9–15). It's His power that controls our dispositions, enables us to serve, and corrects and directs us (see Philippians 2:13). Out of this understanding comes a godly sense of self-worth.

That day marked the intellectual turning point in my spiritual life. The practical working out of that discovery would be lengthy and painful, but at last the realization had come. It was exciting beyond words. I could relax and rest in Jesus. He was going to do the work through me. What peace there was in knowing I could quit struggling!

I soon discovered, however, that my struggles weren't unique. One way or another, many Christians live the way I lived all those years. They've given their hearts to Jesus Christ. They've received Him. They love Him. But they can't seem to make the Christian life work the way they thought it was supposed to work.

Oh, they hang in there. They show up at church. They're part of the twenty per cent who do eighty per cent of the work in most local churches. Or they're part of the sixty per cent who used to be active but now just fill the pews. They have little joy, little freedom, little fruit. In a moment of honesty, they'll admit they're not happy.

You meet unhappy, discouraged, and defeated Christians almost anywhere you go. At least I do. Crest View Church is just one example from many. I have to ask: Is this really what

Jesus had in mind when He came and died on the cross for our sins and rose again and said, 'You shall receive power when the Spirit comes on you, and you shall be my witnesses'? Was this what He expected when he asserted that 'out of your inmost being shall flow rivers of living water'?

Or are some folks missing the whole point?

As I've briefly recounted my spiritual journey, I've alluded to four spiritual truths. These four truths led to my own spiritual renewal. Over the years, as I've travelled around the world, I've taught these four truths extensively and have seen thousands of Christians experience the freeing power of 'Christ in me'.

In the remainder of this book, I want to walk you through these truths. I hope you will open your Bible and take this journey with me. In the process, I hope you will find, like me, that your spiritual passion is rekindled as God radically renews you.

PART TWO

——

*'The work of Christ on the cross for me makes
me safe.
The work of Christ in me makes me happy.'
—John G. Mitchell*

CHAPTER 3

TREMENDOUS POSSIBILITIES

*Let's now begin to look at the biblical principles
of renewal in detail. I pray that God will make
them real in your own life and experience...*

What started out as the internationally acclaimed maiden voyage of the world's largest, most luxurious ship ended as the greatest of sea tragedies when the S.S. Titanic struck an iceberg shortly before midnight April 14, 1912, and went under less than three hours later.

It's said that one-way passage in one of the ship's finest suites cost the equivalent of £25,000 in today's funds. At a length of nearly 883 feet and 66,000 tons displacement, the ship epitomized the word 'titanic' or colossal. Had the ship not met disaster, the S.S. Titanic might have actually added 'unsinkable' as a new meaning the term 'titanic', such were the boasts made about the ship. Instead, most people today who hear the word 'titanic' immediately think of the once mighty ship still lying at the bottom of the Atlantic Ocean some 600 miles off the coast of Nova Scotia.

Ironically, efforts by the S.S. Titanic's crew to avert hitting the now famous iceberg proved disastrous. Had the ship stayed on course, only two or three compartments would have flooded and it would have remained afloat. As it turned out, more than 1,500 people lost their lives.

So much promise. Such needless tragedy. I'm reminded of the S.S. Titanic when I think of the lives of countless hundreds and thousands of people who claim to be Christians but aren't enjoying the Christian life to the hilt. They talk about going to heaven but look like they're having a miserable time here on earth.

Isn't the new life we received in Jesus Christ far better than the old life we supposedly left behind? Think about it. If you're a real Christian, is your future secure? Of course. Are your sins forgiven? Definitely! Are you indwelt by God? Yes!

Yet are you and I enjoying victory over sin these days? Are we holy people? Do others sense the presence of God in our lives? If not, no wonder we lack the courage to share God's Good News with those still outside of Christ. No wonder we sometimes feel the Gospel is only a call to frustration and disillusionment.

The Lord says He's given us His peace, but we still wrestle with worry and restlessness. God commands us to rejoice, but discouragement and depression at times overwhelm us. He tells us to love one another, but we often feel bitter, critical or angry. We're exhorted to glorify the Lord, but when push comes to shove we end up dishonouring Him and feeling guilty instead.

Scripture says that if God is for us, who can be against us? But hardship and tragedy still strike those called by His name. The Bible promises that God gives His children good gifts, but we sometimes feel left out. We read about 'streams of living water' (John 7:38) flowing out of our innermost being, but the joy of the Holy Spirit seldom flows out of our lives.

Is your cup running over this week? Do you feel God is pouring out so many blessings that you don't think you can stand any more? If you're like many Christians I meet, you're probably not saying 'stop blessing me, Lord'; you're quietly aching for a fresh touch of God in your life. You're thinking there must be something more to the Christian life than what you're experiencing.

Do you remember how you felt when you first became a Christian? I could hardly sleep that night, I was so excited about committing my life to Jesus Christ. I knew it was the most important decision I would ever make.

The first days of my Christian life were like the spectacular campfires we built each night at camp, with the flames shooting up towards the sky. But gradually, the inner fire in my soul died. Underneath the ashes of my facade were a few live coals, but from the outside, I appeared cold. After going through a deep spiritual crisis several years later, I finally began to experience, step by step, His renewal in my life. Gradually, kindling and fresh logs were added, the sparks were fanned, and the flame returned. But how I wished that renewal had begun much sooner!

This book is about renewal—how to get the fire of God blazing again in our lives. Renewal is the greatest need in the church today. What is renewal? It's God Himself in action, working in and through us. When we're renewed, our love for God is rekindled. We love His people. The Word of God becomes alive to us again. We gain a vision for evangelism, a burden for the lost. And temptation loses its grip on our affections.

Renewal touches every aspect of our lives. It doesn't depend on carefully orchestrated circumstances or special revival conferences to work us up to some 'mountain top' experience. I'm often reminded of Paul and Nancy Nichols at Crest View. Even though they lost so much—their business, homes, possessions—they actually grew closer to the Lord. Isn't that exactly how someone who is radically renewed should respond?

Some people claim 'I could be happy if life treated me right.' But the fact is: life isn't fair. We all go through rough, sometimes potentially devastating circumstances. Yet the evidence is overwhelming that we can know the joy of the Lord all the same.

I think the problem many Christians have is that they really don't believe in the incredible possibilities available when we experience God's radical renewal. It really is radical—by that, I mean it's fundamental and extreme—compared to the rest of the world. That's why I call the subject of this book 'radical renewal'. I want us to discover what it means to enjoy and keep on enjoying the Christian life, even in life's worst situations.

So what is the potential of radical renewal? We need to see that renewal is a triumphant, victorious life. It is also a transparent, holy life. And it is a total lifestyle dominated by God Himself. Let's take a look at these three tremendous possibilities.

I. Renewal is Triumphant, Victorious Living

We all have different temperaments, different ways we approach life. Some of us are optimistic, others a bit more pessimistic. Some of us are outgoing, others more introverted. Some of us are easygoing, others tend to take life more seriously. Such differences are part of our natural makeup as human beings.

But Scripture teaches that all Christians—whatever their temperament—can be victorious, Spirit-filled, joyful. That's supposed to be the normal Christian life. I love how Paul pictures it: 'Thanks be to God, who in Christ always leads us in triumph, and through us spreads the fragrance of the knowledge of Him everywhere' (2 Corinthians 2:14 RSV).

Notice what Paul says: 'God...leads us in triumph.' And the result? Others sense the fragrance of Christ in our lives. That fragrance permeates the air around any Christian who has experienced radical renewal and who has a passion for the things of God.

The word 'triumph' implies warfare, and we are indeed engaged in spiritual warfare. In this war, one side is going to win and the other side is going to lose. The fact that Christians are led by God in victory doesn't mean we have it easy. It is war out there, and warfare is never pleasant.

Frankly, it's the war raging about us that makes the Christian life exciting, much as a hard fought athletic event is exciting to the athletes who participate. We don't accommodate our foes or pacify them, either. We certainly don't give up when the battle gets fierce. And, in this war, we never accept defeat. We're horrified at that thought. We rebel against it. Instead, we gain victory over our enemies through our Lord Jesus Christ and His victory won on the cross.

Victory Over the World

Scripture speaks of three enemies that we battle. The first of these enemies is the 'world'. I happened to grow up in a church that forever blasted the world. They believed drab was beautiful and that sports and parties were a waste of time. They shunned anything that appeared worldly. I never thought that God's Word might have another perspective.

What does the Bible mean by the world, anyway? As you read the Bible, especially the New Testament, it's amazing how it seems to personify this enemy. When Scripture mentions the world, it isn't talking about this planet. It's describing people on earth who don't know God and, more broadly, their dominating philosophy and way of life.

Though we live in the midst of this present world system, God never intended that we expend all of our energy fighting this one enemy. That was a mistake I saw as I was growing up; we were constantly warned about the evils of certain music, certain people and certain activities. Paradoxically, I found myself so caught up fighting the world that I ended up controlled by the flesh and defeated by the devil.

However, we shouldn't sit around and let the world squeeze us into its mould, either. Many Christians fall for the world because they forget we're at war with it. I don't mean we're at war with the people of this world. We're supposed to love them. But we should hate the whole ugly, arrogant, self-centered, ego-building, pride-engendering system that's out to destroy the lives of those around us.

The world comes at us constantly, even when we're not aware of it. I have a remote control gadget for my television set and can bang through all the channels as I walk through our living room. Sometimes it seems like almost everything that's on, even news and sports, is a pain and a problem. The world is propagating its message from every angle imaginable, twenty-four hours a day. Are we critically interacting with it, or passively accepting any and everything that's thrown at us by the media?

In 1 John 2:15–17 we read: 'Do not love the world or anything in the world. If anyone loves the world, the love of the Father is not in him. For everything in the world—the cravings of sinful man, the lust of his eyes and the boasting of what he has and does—comes not from the Father but from the world. The world and its desires pass away, but the man who does the will of God lives forever.'

Fortunately our victory over the world is sure. Why? Because 'greater is He who is in you than he who is in the world' (1 John 4:4 NASB). The Lord Jesus Himself reminded His disciples: 'In this world you will have trouble. But take heart. I have overcome the world' (John 16:33). So there's a war going on between the desires of the world and the will of God. We all feel it. But we can have victory in that conflict.

All the power of the risen, living Lord Jesus is available to you and me in this war with the world today. That doesn't mean the world's appeal will melt away. We must remember that until we meet the Lord someday, we're still living in enemy territory. But 'though we live in the world, we do not wage war as the world does. The weapons we fight with are not the weapons of the world. On the contrary, they have divine power to demolish strongholds' (2 Corinthians 10:3–4).

What are some of the strongholds of the world? Paul tells us: 'We demolish arguments and every pretension that sets itself up against the knowledge of God, and we take captive every thought to make it obedient to Christ' (2 Corinthians 10:5).

So a stronghold is anything that denies God's rule and authority. We can identify some of the strongholds: attitudes like apathy, materialism, pride and the worship of self. Add to that philosophies like humanism, secularism, and rationalism. Then there are false religions or, as 1 Timothy 4:1 says, the teachings of demons, which are so prevalent today.

These strongholds of the world have an incredible grip on our society, as evidenced in the media, yet they're no match for God's power at work in us. But there's another more subtle enemy we also have to contend with.

Victory Over the Flesh

The second enemy we're at war with is the 'flesh'. Now 'flesh' means more than just our bodies, though our physical frame often is the centre of the battlefield. Some translate this term 'sinful nature'. Others speak of our 'old nature'. In any case, this much is clear: as Christians, we have a terrible enemy entrenched within us.

The flesh is waging war against our soul, opposing the Holy Spirit who indwells us. As Christians, we are exhorted to 'live by the Spirit [so] you will not gratify the desires of the sinful nature. For the sinful nature desires what is contrary to the Spirit, and the Spirit what is contrary to the sinful nature' (Galatians 5:16–17a).

In the very next paragraph of Galatians it's clear that the works of the flesh have no place in the life of the believer. The list is graphic: sexual immorality, impurity and debauchery; idolatry and witchcraft; hatred, discord, jealousy, fits of rage, selfish ambition, dissensions, factions and envy; drunkenness, orgies, and the like. We are warned that 'those who live like this will not inherit the kingdom of God' (Galatians 5:21).

Nevertheless, all of us in the church can be deceived by this enemy. We're easily impressed by good looks, show business and emotional excesses. We're often fooled when the flesh passes itself off as being religious when actually it's acting in a debased or treacherous manner toward others.

In contrast, 'the fruit of the Spirit is love, joy, peace, patience, kindness, goodness, faithfulness, gentleness and self-control. Against such things there is no law' (Galatians 5:22–

23). Why isn't there a law against the fruit of the Spirit? Because we can never love too much, or have too much joy or peace. But even this world, as corrupt and fallen as it is, puts limits on the acts of the flesh.

There's a very real battle within us. If we give in to the lusts of the flesh, we automatically grieve the Holy Spirit and quench His work within us. But that doesn't have to remain the case in our lives. We can know victory on this battlefront, too! Paul reminds us that 'we have an obligation—but it is not to the sinful nature, to live according to it' (Romans 8:12).

Someone who is younger may think, 'Hey, Luis, you're older now. Of course you can talk about having victory in this area. At your age you should. But I've got blood in my veins. I've got temptations. And the flesh drags me down.'

Don't think only the young and single struggle with the lusts of the flesh. I promise, the temptations go on all your life. Every day I still have to confront my sinful nature. We're all at war with this enemy. It's what destroys many Christians. But it doesn't have to. Are you experiencing victory over the flesh? By the power of the Holy Spirit your answer can be an emphatic 'yes'!

Victory Over the Devil

There's a third enemy—the devil. The Bible also calls him Satan, Lucifer, the adversary, and the deceiver. A lot of people, even in Christian circles, paint a caricature of him and think he's laughable. But, as we all find out sooner or later, the devil is a vicious enemy of our souls.

The Lord Jesus put it bluntly: 'He [the devil] was a murderer from the beginning, not holding to the truth, for there is no truth in him. When he lies, he speaks his native language, for he is a liar and the father of lies' (John 8:44).

The difference between Satan and Christ couldn't be greater. 'The thief [again referring to the devil] comes only to steal and kill and destroy; I have come that they may have life, and have it to the full' (John 10:10).

Satan's lies and murderous intentions aren't aimed at non-Christians only. He has already veiled the eyes of those who are perishing (2 Corinthians 4:4). Rather, his fiercest anger and rage is directed against those who have been rescued from his dominion of darkness.

Peter warns us, 'Your enemy the devil prowls around like a roaring lion looking for someone to devour. Resist him, standing firm in the faith, because you know that your brothers throughout the world are undergoing the same kind of sufferings' (1 Peter 5:8–9). James adds, 'Resist the devil, and he will flee from you. Come near to God and he will come near to you. Wash your hands, you sinners, and purify your hearts, you double-minded' (James 4:7–8). Paul urges us to put on spiritual armour in order to protect ourselves from this enemy: 'Be strong in the Lord and in his mighty power. Put on the full armor of God so that you can take your stand against the devil's schemes. For our struggle is not against flesh and blood, but against the rulers, against the authorities, against the powers of this dark world and against the spiritual forces of evil in heavenly realms. Therefore put on the full armor of God, so that when the day of evil comes, you may be able to stand your ground, and after you have done everything, to stand' (Ephesians 6:10–13).

There's no demilitarized zone in the midst of this war. Either we're standing in the strength of God's power or we're knocked down in defeat. There's no room for pride, for thinking we can walk a line somewhere between the kingdom of darkness and the kingdom of light.

Are you living in victory against the devil? Can you say, 'Thanks be to God, who in Christ always leads us in triumph'? Or are you experiencing failure and defeat? Absolute perfection is impossible until we get to heaven, but we can experience ongoing victory over the world, the flesh and the devil. That's the first great possibility before us.

II. Renewal is Transparent, Holy Living

Scripture also teaches that the Christian life is a transparent, holy life. The Bible says, 'As obedient children, do not conform to the evil desires you had when you lived in ignorance. But just as he who called you is holy, so be holy in all you do; for it is written, "Be holy, because I am holy" ' (1 Peter 1:14–16).

The Bible also says, 'Make every effort to live in peace with all men and to be holy; without holiness no one will see the Lord' (Hebrews 12:14). And John reminds us, 'If we walk in the light, as he is in the light, we have fellowship with one another, and the blood of Jesus, his Son, purifies us from all sin' (1 John 1:7).

What does it mean to be holy and transparent? Holiness means to live in the light with God. It means to walk in accordance with all that we've learned in the Word as the Holy Spirit teaches us. In other words, it's a commitment to purity.

Transparency means that, as far as I know, I don't have anything to hide from my heavenly Father. Further, there is nothing between me and anyone else that I haven't tried to settle from my side of things—even if the other person doesn't want to settle the issue.

Holiness isn't a movement or annual convention; it can be our vital, daily experience. Transparency doesn't mean absolute perfection, though that is the goal. We must never lower the standard the Lord Jesus gave us as His disciples: 'Be perfect, therefore, as your heavenly Father is perfect' (Matthew 5:48). We must never accommodate sin, even though we sometimes fail the Lord. However, a proper realization of our imperfection doesn't need to lead to despair.

Some of God's holiest and most honoured servants in years gone by actually became more aware of their imperfections as they drew closer to the Lord. They lamented their sinfulness, even though they weren't committing any terrible, wicked deeds of the flesh. Instead, as the Holy Spirit scrutinized their lives, they saw even their smallest faults as massive sins. And they longed for the day of Christ when God's good work within them would be complete (Philippians 1:6) and they would be holy like Jesus (1 John 3:2).

You see this in Paul's descriptions of himself. Toward the end of his life, he called himself the worst of sinners (1 Timothy 1:15). That wasn't hyperbole; that was based on objective fact. Paul had ransacked the church and committed the most violent of crimes before his conversion.

But he also rejoiced in God's complete forgiveness and actively pursued holiness. Paul could say, 'Not that I have...already been made perfect, but I press on to take hold of that for which Christ Jesus took hold of me' (Philippians 3:12). Lack of perfection didn't stop Paul from living as transparently as possible. Why? Because he was conscious of the fear of the Lord, and because he longed for the day when he would see his Lord face to face.

Are you holy? Am I holy? Are we enjoying the freedom of a transparent conscience? Can we honestly say, 'Lord, I praise Your name that there's nothing to hide from You. I'm not covering up anything. I'm walking in the light. My soul is clean. My conscience is transparent. As far as I know, there's nothing I need to settle with anyone. Lord, I love You and I thank You there isn't a cloud between You and me.'

Such a statement is your privilege as a Christian. It's the great offer of the Gospel. The point of Christianity, to a great measure, is that God loves us and wants us to enjoy the freedom of relating to Him in holiness and transparency. His delight is that we walk in the light, that we live holy and happy in Him. Is that our experience, or is something getting in the way?

Today we're bombarded by the world and its way of thinking. We're continually enticed to cross the line, to give in to the flesh, to pledge alliance to the devil. Often we're not even aware of what's happening.

The world is great at promoting its own agenda and ideas. Men and women make careers out of listening to people's problems and offering advice. Others write newspaper col-

umns or appear on talk shows. And sometimes what they
have to say sounds pretty good.

But good advice isn't good enough. God's Good News is
the radical power of the Lord Jesus Christ. He doesn't offer
us advice; He offers us power to live holy and transparently in
a corrupt and deceitful age.

Now I know some people react and say, 'Come on! I've
heard all this talk before. Victorious Christian living? What a
cliché! Walking in the light with a clear conscience? What a
joke! You can try to make it sound good, but it doesn't work
for me.'

When a person says something like that, it reveals two
things about his or her character. First, that person doesn't
have a clear conscience. And second, he or she has become
cynical. Cynicism is the language of the devil, and it leads to
depression.

It shouldn't surprise us that many cynical saints are
depressed. The fragrance of Christ is missing in their lives.
They've lost their first love for the Lord. They've lost the joy
and peace Christ brings. In place of a passion for the lost,
they've become critical or at least sceptical of the Church and
the things of God.

Thankfully, God has provided a mechanism for forgiveness
if our conscience is contaminated. We'll consider that in more
detail later. First, there's one more tremendous possibility of
the Christian life to consider.

III. Renewal is a Total Lifestyle

Scripture teaches that the Christian life is a total lifestyle
dominated by God Himself. To me, this is the most exciting
possibility imaginable. No wonder Paul prayed earnestly that
'out of his [the Father's] glorious riches he may strengthen
you with power through his Spirit in your inner being, so that
Christ may dwell in your hearts through faith' (Ephesians
3:16–17).

Listen to the rest of Paul's prayer: 'And I pray that you,

being rooted and established in love, may have power, together with all the saints [and that includes you and me], to grasp how wide and long and high and deep is the love of Christ, and to know this love that surpasses knowledge—that you may be filled to the measure of all the fullness of God' (Ephesians 3:14–19).

Did you catch that last phrase? 'That you may be filled to the measure of all the fullness of God.' Imagine how different your life would be if you were completely, totally filled with God Himself. No area of your life would be untouched. You would love God so much more deeply. You would care so much more about your brothers and sisters in Christ. And you would have such a passion for souls.

The whole purpose of the Christian life is that God take over more and more of our lives. That He mould His character in us. That we become like His Son, Jesus Christ. That's what radical renewal is all about. But that isn't the experience of most Christians. And it isn't what the world sees when it looks at most people in the Church today.

When people look at you and me, what do they see? Do they see God in us? The thing that haunts me the most is the thought that a news reporter would ask my wife and close friends, 'What is Luis Palau really like?' and they would say, 'He's a phony. He talks about the power of God, but I don't see any of it in his life.' That would kill me.

What really counts is this: Does God run my life? Is He in control? Or am I trying to run the show?

Do people see God in your life and in mine? Is every area of our lives dominated and filled with God Himself? Painfully, the answer is sometimes 'No.' In the next chapter we'll briefly examine the reason why.

To Ponder

1. In this chapter I remarked that 'We sometimes feel the Gospel is only a call to frustration and disillusionment.' What expectations did you have when you became a Christian?

Were you ever disappointed? What expectations do you have now?

2. 'This book is about renewal—how to get the fire of God blazing again in our lives. What is renewal? It's God Himself in action, working in and through us.' Have you ever experienced renewal? What prompted it? What was it like?

3. 'Until we meet the Lord someday, we're still living in enemy territory.' In what ways does the world try to squeeze you into its mould of thinking and behaving? What is your best defence?

4. 'The flesh is waging war against our soul, opposing the Holy Spirit who indwells us.' Do you feel like you struggle with the lusts of the flesh more now than when you first became a Christian, or less? Why do you think that is?

5. 'As we all find out sooner or later, the devil is a vicious enemy.' Is it possible to escape his attacks? How? What have you experienced?

6. 'The point of Christianity, in a great measure, is that God loves us and wants us to enjoy the freedom of relating to Him in holiness and transparency.' Do you agree or disagree? Why do you feel that way?

7. 'Imagine how different your life would be if you were completely, totally filled with God Himself.' How would it be different in your relationship to God? In your relationships with others? In your attitude toward those without Christ?

To Pursue

1. As I mentioned in 'How to Use This Book', don't stop to do these exercises until after you've read this book through once. Then complete each step in the order recommended.

2. In this chapter, I've tried to whet your appetite and start you dreaming about enjoying the tremendous possibilities of the Christian life. But I haven't suggested any course of action yet. So allow me to address the important issue of what it means to be a Christian.

3. Have you trusted Jesus Christ as your Saviour? If so, take out your notebook and a pen. Title the first page 'What Christ has done in my life so far.' Write a couple of paragraphs to describe the difference He's made in your life. Try to be specific.

4. If you can't think of many things Christ has done in your life, jot down in your notebook what you might have done if He hadn't saved you.

5. If you haven't trusted Jesus Christ as Saviour yet, or if you aren't sure whether you have, I would encourage you to read my booklet *What Is a Real Christian?* (CWR).

CHAPTER 4

WHY ARE WE MISSING OUT?

There's only one thing that can keep us from enjoying the Christian life to the fullest possible extent....

When Air Canada took delivery of four Boeing 767s several years back, the new jumbo jets were the pride of the fleet. That is, until Flight 143 from Montreal to Edmonton one fateful Monday.

After a short hop from Montreal to Ottawa, Captain Robert Pearson and co-pilot Marcel Quintal manoeuvred Flight 143 back into the air for the 2,000-mile trip to Edmonton. Passengers were enjoying a movie when the jumbo jet's massive engines abruptly stopped.

Only those without earphones noticed at first. Then came a break in the movie. Captain Pearson announced that Flight 143 would be making an emergency landing. Sixty-nine people were trapped in an agonizingly slow but inescapable descent to earth.

For several minutes, a desperate silence hung over the cabin. Then fear gave way to screams as the crash-landing neared. All the latest technology couldn't keep the jumbo jet in the air another second longer.

Eight hundred miles short of its destination, Flight 143 had run out of fuel. Anyone could have made the same mistake. The electronic digital fuel gauge on the Boeing 767 was out of order so—as the rules permit— Captain Pearson and co-pilot

Quintal had relied on figures given by the refuelling crew before takeoff.

But someone on the refuelling crew had confused pounds for kilograms. Somewhere over Winnipeg the truth came out. The jumbo jet should have still had 26,760 pounds of fuel left. It had none.

By God's grace, Captain Pearson and co-pilot Quintal were able to glide Flight 143 some 100 miles to an ex-military air field Quintal remembered with uncanny detail from his air force days. A dramatic crash landing heavily damaged the jumbo jet's landing gear, but no one on board was hurt. That isn't always the case.

Multiplied thousands of Christians right now are in a desperate Flight 143 situation. They know it's possible to live a victorious and holy life, one filled with God Himself. But they aren't living on that level. Instead, they're slowly gliding toward earth—weighed down with dissatisfaction, discouragement and defeat. Their efforts to regain spiritual momentum have proved anything but effective, and they're deathly afraid of what's next.

Why do we see so many spiritual disasters? Why do we suffer so many unnecessary battles? Why so much depression? Why so much carnality?

I've heard all kinds of excuses. If you're a counsellor or small-group leader or deacon or elder or pastor, you've probably heard many of these same excuses, too. 'Times are tough financially.' 'It's hard to play it straight in the business world.' 'With all the openness about sexuality these days, what am I supposed to do?' 'I just don't love my wife any more, so why should I stay with her?' 'I know I should spend more time reading the Bible, but with the demands of work and all, well, I also need time just to relax.'

People talk as if there's no way in the world to walk in the light of God's Word, by His Spirit. 'I want to be holy, but the media make it so tough. We live in such a sensual society. How can anyone stay pure any more?'

Admittedly, the world is a very unholy place. Malcolm

Muggeridge says the crisis of our day isn't political or eco-
nomic or ecological but 'the loss of a sense of moral order'.
Richard Halverson says 'moral, ethical anarchy' is ransacking
Western society. Relativism reigns supreme.

But even if we did live in a godly society, there would be
other excuses. 'If you knew my spouse, you wouldn't talk
about the victorious Christian life. I invite you to be a guest at
our house for a week, Luis, then tell me how victorious you
feel.' Or 'My mother-in-law is staying with us and until she
goes home, believe me, there isn't any victory in our house.'
Or 'You don't know how tough it is in my job. I can't be
honest and survive.'

People can make any excuse they want, but let me say this
with authority from God's Word. No one can take away the
anointing of the Holy Spirit from our lives. No one can keep
our cup from running over. No one can steal the joy of the
Lord from us. Not our in-laws. Not our spouse. Not our
boss. Not even Satan. No one! No matter how ugly they are
or how big a pain they may be. And some people are a pain.

There's only one thing that can keep you and me from
enjoying the Christian life to the fullest extent possible. Sin.
There's no one else to blame. This is the negative side of
radical renewal: we have to acquire a new vision of sin. We
need to recognize that sin acts like a deadly spiritual cancer
within our souls.

If you and I want to experience all the tremendous possibilities of the Christian life, we can! The only thing that
makes us bitter, or frustrated, or defeated, or ugly, or dark, or
a pain to others, is sin.

Sin is a horrible subject. But unless we are completely right
with God and have nothing to confess to Him, we must face
this issue squarely. Solemnly, we need to speak the truth
before the Lord.

The Need to Undergo Divine Surgery

If you took your spouse or best friend to the doctor because he or she had discovered a potentially cancerous growth, what would you expect the doctor to say? 'Take two aspirin and call me in the morning'? No way! If he said that to me, I'd storm out and never come back. If the situation is serious, I want the doctor to tell me the truth. What is this lump? We need to know. If it's bad, we want it out.

My wife Pat and I actually faced this trial several years ago. Pat discovered a lump, so we immediately took her to the doctor. He determined the lump was cancerous, so radical surgery was scheduled for the next Monday. Then months, actually years of recovery followed. What if we'd ignored the doctor's findings and cancelled the surgery? The consequences, almost certainly, would have been disastrous. Sure the surgery and treatment was painful, but it was better than losing my wife.

Like a doctor getting ready to operate on a cancer patient, I hate to deal with the subject of sin. But it has to be done. If you and I are living with any form of sin in our hearts, it's deadly. Unless we undergo God's divine surgery, sin will grow ever more malignant within our souls. The Lord's work in and through us eventually will be squelched. We can't go on day after day, year after year as if nothing is wrong.

We need to ask God to examine our hearts. Our prayer can be that of the psalmist: 'Search me, O God, and know my heart; try me and know my anxieties; and see if there is any wicked way in me...' (Psalm 139:23–24 NKJV).

It's not enough to pretend we're walking with the Lord. How sensitive are we to sin? Are we indulging in talk and activities that defile our soul? If so, we are grieving the Holy Spirit even if we don't sense it. Sometimes it takes a while before we realize, 'I have lost the joy. I used to be so happy in the Lord. What happened?'

We need to ask God to make us increasingly sensitive to sin. That's especially important in the culture in which we live today. Moral standards have been knocked down and kicked around. Ethics are now being decided by preference and public opinion.

In such days, I find this prayer of commitment incredibly relevant and challenging: 'I will walk in my house with blameless heart. I will set before my eyes no vile thing. The deeds of faithless men I hate; they will not cling to me. Men of perverse heart shall be far from me; I will have nothing to do with evil' (Psalm 101:2b–4).

According to Scripture, there must not be even a hint of immorality or impurity in our lives. We're to have no partnership with the ungodly, and nothing to do with the fruitless deeds of darkness (Ephesians 5:3–11).

What hints of sin, what deeds of darkness are lodged within our soul? I tremble at the thought of even discussing this subject. I certainly can't point an accusing finger at you; I'm a sinner like everyone else. But I've experienced God's divine surgery, and I know how important it is to go through this process.

Pinpointing Unconfessed Sins

The secret of ongoing, continuous renewal is brokenness and repentance. We humbly need to ask the Holy Spirit to search our hearts repeatedly. Is our conscience clear right now, or is it contaminated? Do we need to admit any weaknesses or failures?

This process of examination takes more than a moment's reflection, but can begin at any time. It may take place during the sermon next Sunday. It can start when we're quietly reading the Bible tomorrow morning. The process may even begin before we're finished with this chapter. I know God wants to speak to my heart as I write about this subject. Ask Him to speak to you as you continue reading.

When God does begin to speak to us, the temptation is to think immediately of someone else. If a sermon gets too convicting, we say to ourselves, 'I hope Mrs. Smith is listening right now!' Or we begin to read something powerful but then give it to someone else to take the pressure off us. Rather than thinking about others who need this message, let's ask God to speak to our hearts right now during the next few minutes.

Drifting into Moral Indifference

Christians never fall into gross sin overnight. Sin usually encroaches an inch at a time. One minor disobedience because of a lack of dedication and surrender eventually leads to other things. C.S. Lewis has said that our big choices for good or evil are conditioned by 'private little choices' made along the way.

Those private little choices can end up redirecting the whole course of our life. People who shipwreck their lives never intended to steer so far off course. It was a little deception here, a little white lie there, tiny things along the way that lowered their moral and spiritual sensitivity and sent them drifting toward a massive catastrophe.

Let's think about the private little choices we've made. Have you begun to drift into a sea of indifference without realizing it? Please don't gloss over the next few pages. Instead, ask God to search your heart as you think through some common areas of compromise.

Absorbed with Self

Today everybody's talking about self-acceptance, self-actualization, self-advancement, self-affirmation, self-awareness, self-esteem, self-fulfilment, self-gratification, self-image, self-importance, self-improvement, self-perception, self-satisfaction, self-sufficiency, self-understanding, self-worth.

Of course you recognize the common denominator in all these. Yet what is the greatest enemy of the fullness of the Spirit? Self.

Our culture subscribes to the cult of self. We're bombarded by its propaganda through newspaper and magazine articles, radio and television programmes, and endless advertisements.

The world talks about self all the time, and it's easy for us to talk this way, too.

Recently I heard about a pastor's wife who went to an exercise dance class to lose a little weight. One reason for going, she said, was to be herself. The place was jammed with divorced women who complained that men are 'a bunch of pigs', 'indifferent', and 'unfulfilling'. This woman, a pastor's wife, bought into it and eventually walked out on her husband. Why? Primarily because she became completely focused on herself.

You and I can fall into the same trap. We can justify our absorption with self. We can explain it away. We can use any argument we want, but it's destroying marriages and homes. Self absorption needlessly diverts people from true meaning and purpose in life.

Repeating Gossip

You might be thinking, 'Come on, Luis. Deal with some of the big sins.' This is a heavy one. Most of us are not about to commit adultery—if nothing else, out of fear of God. But what hurts Christian families and congregations more than almost anything else? People who gossip, saying things that shouldn't be repeated.

Gossip isn't telling a lie about someone else. That's slander. Gossip is when we learn something that's probably true about someone and we repeat it when we know we shouldn't. We all have this tendency, and people love to pull it out of us. And we love to draw it out of others.

Some people are magnets for gossip. They know things Scotland Yard hasn't even discovered yet. You might be friends with someone like that, and every time you talk to that person you end up feeling dirty. It's tough to stop someone from telling us all that garbage, isn't it? It's even harder to forget it instead of passing it on to someone else. But Scripture says to get rid of this sin. This, too, has to be confessed.

Harbouring Unbelief

This may be the most serious and devastating sin of all. If we're cynical, we wouldn't dare admit it to our parents or spouse or children. But in our hearts, we sit back and question what the Word of God clearly teaches. What dishonour that brings to the Lord.

Take the Lord's command to 'seek first his [God's] kingdom and his righteousness' and His promise that 'all these things [material needs] will be given to you as well' (Matthew 6:33). This is one of my favourite verses, one I often write when a child asks me to sign his or her Bible. I love that verse, I believe it, I know it's true and for more than forty years my life has proved it. Nevertheless, how many times have I despaired over financial or other needs? The Lord has never failed me, but I still sometimes panic and distrust Him. That's committing the sin of unbelief.

Or take the promise that 'sin shall not have dominion over you, for you are not under law but under grace' (Romans 6:14 NKJV). Now someone can argue that this verse isn't a promise, or that only pietists and 'holiness' folks really believe it. That's an insult to God. It's like having your best friend mention she is buying you a terrific gift only to have you snarl back, 'Forget it. That's ridiculous. I don't believe you for a second. You have no intention of getting me any such gift.' You might be right after a response like that. Your friend would be hurt and upset at you, and rightly so. Do we insult God the same way by refusing to believe His promises?

Is there cynicism in your soul? Is there contempt for the clear-cut, revealed promises of God? Do you hear about the possibilities of the Christian life and say, 'Sure, go ahead, talk about it all you want. But I know better'? Bring that unbelief to the cross of Christ today.

Unthankful Spirit

Many Christians enjoy material blessings. But it's so easy to complain about what we don't have instead of praising God for all the good things He has given to us.

Many years ago when my wife and I were preparing to be missionaries, our salary was a few hundred dollars a month. It definitely didn't seem like enough for a family of four. But we were rejoicing that the Lord was providing for all of our needs. Another missionary heard my praise and snapped, 'Come on, Luis. You're from South America, so anything is a big deal to you. But this is not enough money for a guy to survive.'

I kept my mouth shut, but I never forgot that fellow's remarks. Today he's divorced and chasing his own dreams instead of serving God. He was a thankless Christian. Instead of saying, 'Lord, thank You that I'm healthy; I have something to eat; I've got clothes to wear,' he complained about what he didn't have.

I believe thanklessness is a great sin against the Lord. Maybe you haven't succeeded like you thought you were going to when you entered the work world. Maybe you're having a rough time of it at home. But if you forget to thank God for His goodness to you, even in the midst of your problems, you grieve Him. You quench the Holy Spirit's work in your life and you keep yourself from His further blessing in your life.

Feeling Resentful

Since our culture has made materialism almost a religion, it's extremely easy to become resentful. My grandparents were from Europe, but I happened to grow up in Argentina. My family became fairly well off, thanks to my dad's hard work, wise planning and the blessing of the Lord on his life.

Then my dad died unexpectedly at the age of thirty-five. Within three years our family was living in poverty, to the point where we couldn't pay our rent for eight months. It was only the mercy of our landlord that he didn't throw us out on the street.

Despite our poverty, my mother never became resentful. She almost made a point of saying 'Isn't that exciting?' whenever we heard about someone going on an expensive holiday or buying something extravagant. She never complained: 'Why, they know I'm a widow with six children. They should know we're destitute. Why don't they give us the money instead?'

My mother taught us never to become resentful toward others. Some nights she had nothing more than a loaf of French bread with a little garlic to serve seven people for dinner. Yet my mother always rejoiced, and she gladly celebrated with others. Her attitude was a fantastic example to me.

Scripture doesn't just say 'mourn with those who mourn' but also 'rejoice with those who rejoice' (Romans 12:15). Resentment is an awful sin. Even out of enlightened self-interest, it's best to rejoice. Resentment only makes you a very dislikable person. So rejoice with those who rejoice. Do it because the Lord says so and because it's the godly thing to do. Get into the habit of rejoicing with others out loud, especially if you feel a tinge of resentment.

Making Petty Complaints

I have seen many revivals during more than twenty-five years of ministry. My first was at a church in Colombia where I was serving as a missionary-evangelist. That revival was nearly destroyed by a petty complaint.

Two weeks into the revival, one of the church elders stood to speak during a service. Apparently there had been a mix-up. This elder had spent the equivalent of, say, £10 on flowers, but someone else's flowers were used to decorate the pulpit area instead.

'This isn't fair,' the elder complained. 'It was my turn to buy the flowers. What about all the money I've just spent?'

Now this was in front of everyone, including dozens of new believers in the congregation. That single attitude over something irrelevant and forgettable stirred up needless trouble and almost ruined the meeting.

Often it's the little things that kill the joy of the Lord among us, isn't it? A series of little things left unconfessed and accumulated can devastate us and those around us.

Before my wife and I left for our first missionary term overseas, we were sent by our mission board to visit a church that was having a business meeting that Sunday night. We were sitting on one side of the church. The pastor and fretful wife were seated up front. You could sense trouble coming.

As the meeting started, someone stood and said, 'I feel that our pastor...' and she laid out her complaint. Then a man got up and said, 'I agree with Mrs. Smith. The pastor has done this and that.' Now the pastor hadn't committed sin. They were complaining about petty baloney, but they made a big deal out of it.

Suddenly a teenage girl in the back stood up and began to cry. 'What are you people doing? Why are you trying to hurt my dad? He's a wonderful man. He loves you all. He prays for you every morning. I've heard him cry for you in his office. Why are you saying all these things about him?' Whew! I thought. How wicked Christians can be. The things we say about other Christians. Of course they made mistakes, but don't we all? How can we be so wicked?

Neglected Giving

If one were to look at the percentage of Christians who give any significant amount for local evangelism or missions overseas, it would appear that nearly eighty-five per cent are indifferent to the Great Commission. That's incredible when you think how much God has blessed us materially.

We actually miss out on the further blessing of God when we neglect to give to evangelism, missions and the ongoing ministry of our local church. Jesus said, 'Give, and it will be given to you. A good measure, pressed down, shaken together and running over, will be poured into your lap. For with the measure you use, it will be measured to you' (Luke 6:38). We're to give ourselves 100 per cent to the Lord, then give generously and cheerfully from our substance.

When my wife and I were serving in Latin America, my giving tended to be spontaneous and, therefore, sporadic. If I saw or heard about a need, I would respond 'as the Lord leads'. Then the Lord taught me the joy of giving regularly and sacrificially.

I feel truly blessed now when I give to my local church and when I send gifts to people serving the Lord in various parts of the world. It's a fantastic joy. Is that your experience yet? Or is this an area to confess to the Lord?

Ignoring Recurring Sins

Some people have no problem enjoying victory over the temptation to lie or lose their temper, but they struggle with lust. Lust has become a recurring sin in their life. For others, their recurring sin may be covetousness, envy, jealousy or some other area.

We all have at least one besetting sin, a sin that keeps tripping us up (Hebrews 12:1). We can end up feeling almost obsessed by it. 'Why can't I defeat this sin?' we ask. 'Why does this particular temptation always plague me?' Satan attacks us in other areas, of course, but we shouldn't be surprised that he concentrates on our area of weakness.

For our spiritual health and well-being, it's critical that we identify our recurring sin by name. We don't want to reinforce such sin by always talking about it or thinking about it. But until we name our recurring sin, and take necessary steps to overcome it (which I'll talk about later), we'll keep on giving in to it and feeling more and more frustrated and defeated by it.

What is your recurring sin? Have you confessed it to the Lord? Have you made a list of realistic steps to take to avoid it in the future? Have you asked a spiritually mature Christian friend to keep you accountable? Are you actively avoiding places of temptation? Are you on your guard against pride after each victory?

Beware of falling into the trap of thinking, 'I've gone too far. I'm trapped. I'll never have victory over this sin again.' As we'll see in chapter seven, God's power at work within you can completely liberate you from any and all sin.

I've seen God liberate alcoholics, prostitutes, cold-blooded murderers, and little old ladies with dirty rotten attitudes by the power of the reality that 'Christ lives in me'. He can do the same in your life!

Lacking True Joy

Do you lack a genuine sense of joy? Yes, that's a sin, too. After all, we're commanded to 'Rejoice in the Lord always. I will say it again: Rejoice!' (Philippians 4:4). Yet a lack of joy often marks our lives as Christians. Years ago, I had to identify the lack of joy for what it is—one of my recurring sins.

God doesn't want us to be flighty, shallow clowns with silly grins painted on our faces. Clowns are all right for circuses, but God commands us to be genuinely joyful day in and day out. That doesn't mean we don't experience trials and hardships. But in the midst of those trials and hardships, we can rejoice. After all, the apostle Paul wrote his commands to 'rejoice!' while sitting in a Roman jail.

Some people have remarked, 'I may not look happy on the outside, but deep down inside I have great joy.' Sometimes that's hard to swallow. There should be evidence of joy. I don't believe there's a difference between true happiness and joy, though you may disagree with me on that point.

Sexual Impurity

This is a delicate subject, but if we don't face this issue, it can destroy us. King David learned this the hard way by committing adultery with the wife of one of his generals and then having that general killed. David paid the consequences for the rest of his life. But I believe David's problem began long before the act of adultery, when he was young.

In studying David's life, I've become convinced he never dealt with this issue before the Lord. David talked to God about whether to go to war against the Philistines or refrain from battle. He cried out to God in his distress and he praised God for His goodness. As far as I can tell, David prayed about almost every area except his sexual temptation, which happened to be one of his areas of recurring sin. He ended up an embarrassed old man when he could have finished victoriously.

I'm long into the Christian life now, and I think I've seen it all. But today there is a duplicity when it comes to sexuality. Instead of holding to God's standard of purity, professing Christians are committing fornication, adultery, even homosexuality. It's bad enough that such things are happening, but some Christians are even trying to justify such sinful behaviour.

What God forbids and says He hates we often hear discussed with such light-heartedness. It shocks the world and shakes the younger generation in our churches. And then we wonder why there's no blessing. Why there's no power. Why there's no joy. Why there's no victory. Why there's no revival and renewal. It's because there is no holiness. I hate to talk about this, but we can't ignore reality.

I think men may have it just a bit rougher than most women when it comes to dealing with sexual temptation. Are you tempted to thumb through magazines with suggestive or pornographic pictures? Are you tempted to watch immorality on the screen? If you're giving in to such temptation, go to the Lord and confess your sins now.

I've seen friends, including some in the ministry, destroy themselves because of sexual impurity. And I've helped counsel countless others who have experienced grief caused by immorality and infidelity.

The Bible says those who are committed to Christ have crucified the flesh with its passions and desires (Galatians 5:24). God wants us to deal radically and ruthlessly with sin. There's no room for pampering or playing around.

Feeling Bitter

A friend of mine went through a massive emotional breakdown. After his recovery, we went for a walk. 'Luis,' he told me, 'don't allow anyone to ever make you bitter. My problems began when I got worked up about the contractor who didn't build my basement and driveway right. I hated what he'd done to my home. And since he lived next door, I saw him almost every day. Each time I saw him, my anger and bitterness grew even more intense until I finally cracked.'

No wonder God's Word is clear: 'Get rid of all bitterness' (Ephesians 4:31). Why? Because if a 'bitter root grows up' within you, it will 'cause trouble and defile many' (Hebrews 12:15).

Not everybody suffers a massive emotional breakdown from unresolved bitterness, but I've met many people who have allowed it to poison their lives. A young woman came up to me in Scotland after I had preached about parent-child relationships. 'I can't obey my father,' she said. 'He's gone to Saudi Arabia for three years. He never comes home. I refuse to honour and obey him.' She was clearly angry and bitter against her father.

After we'd talked for a while, I said, 'Look, the Bible says honour and obey your father, whether you feel like it or not.' I advised her to write to her father and honestly say how hurt she felt that he didn't come home or write or call very often. I also urged her to confess her bitterness, then tell her father that she would honour and obey him from now on in obedience to God's Word.

Several months later I received a note from this young Scottish woman. 'I've never felt so free as when I followed your advice and wrote that letter. In fact, because of that letter, my father did come home. He asked forgiveness from my mother and me, and our family is reconciled once again.'

What happens if we don't deal with bitterness in our soul? Eventually, we become bitter at God Himself. This is one of the most shocking sins imaginable. People actually shake their fists and angrily shout, 'God, why did you let this happen?'

When my wife got cancer, we told people that there are two ways of asking 'Why?' There is the bitter, defiant 'Why?' And there is the intelligent, understanding 'Why?' One is blasphemy. The other is an appropriate, Christian response to the hardships of life.

Many times I prayed while my wife was going through all the rigours of surgery and chemotherapy: 'Why is this happening, Lord? What am I supposed to learn from this? Is there any reason why it happened? Is there anything that we as a family need to learn? Is there anything I need to learn in order to minister to others more effectively?'

That's completely different from, 'God, I'm mad at You. Why the h— did you allow my wife to come down with cancer? We've got four boys....' Such outbursts reveal a bitter heart. That anger should be decisively dealt with.

Some Christian counsellors and psychologists have actively suggested that people vent their angry feelings toward God. Since when is God to blame? Yet this form of blasphemy is being justified in numerous articles and books. That doesn't make it any less of a sin.

It's easy to blame God for the wickedness of others. I've had to endure vicious criticism and attacks over the years, unjust accusations from the enemies of the Gospel. People have tried to destroy me and my ministry in certain countries. It hurts. By nature I want to hit back. It's not fair. But the minute I get angry and bitter, I grieve the Holy Spirit.

If you're bitter against someone, or angry at God, don't play games. Ask God to perform divine surgery. Get on your knees beside your bed or wherever you can pray alone and confess your bitterness by name. Tell the whole story to the

Lord. Yes, the Lord already knows all the details, but confess it anyway. Admit your sins to Him.

Clearing the Slate

It's time to do business with God. Ask God to search your heart right now. Get alone and take a sheet of paper and pen. On the top left-hand side write: 'Things I must get right with God.' On the top right-hand side: 'Things I must clear up with other people.'

Now in the left-hand column write down any sins God shows you, whatever they may be. We've considered only a few in this chapter. We could have picked a hundred others that Scripture addresses: sins like impatience, worry, pride, self-righteousness, independence, laziness, greed, substance abuse, carelessness, divisiveness, disloyalty, demandingness, prayerlessness, neglect of the Lord's Supper, or lack of commitment to the local church.

Ask God to do a deep work in your soul. Write down every sin you're guilty of, whether it takes half a sheet of paper or half a dozen pages. Don't rush. Don't assume you don't have any unconfessed sins. Why let them keep piling up because you're always in a hurry? Take time out to be quiet before the Lord, away from distractions. Allow Him to examine every area of your life. If you're serious, He won't hesitate to convict you of specific sins.

As you list the sins, in the right-hand column write the names of anyone you've hurt, deceived, been bitter against, gossiped about, failed to show love and compassion to, cheated, or whatever the offence might be.

If you're young, perhaps you improperly broke off a friendship or dating relationship with someone. You hurt that person but have never asked for forgiveness. Or maybe your relationship with a parent, sibling or your spouse is strained. Have you admitted what you've done wrong? Are you actively seeking reconciliation? Have you forgiven them even if they won't be reconciled to you?

Is there someone to whom you owe restitution? Perhaps you've cheated in a business deal or let a debt go bad. Like Zacchaeus the tax collector, maybe you've taken advantage of people. Are you willing to break that cycle of sin? Do you want to make things right?

A university student came to me once and said, 'Luis, if I listed everything, I figure I'd have to write down about 500 things.' So I asked him, 'What's the biggest thing you've done that you need to make right?' He admitted that one night after a football game in high school, he and three friends blew up a petrol station, and destroyed three cars, too. I told this young man that he had to confess this to God, then go and make restitution. 'I could never pay for that,' he objected, but he already was paying for it, inside. He had become suicidal. Sin was eating away at his soul.

We can't afford to delay God's divine surgery in our lives, even if surgery is painful, because the cancer of sin never stops growing. So take time now before the Lord and let Him speak to your heart. Write down any known sins, and ask God to reveal your hidden faults, too. Write them all down, but don't put your name on the list or leave it around for anyone else to see.

As you write out your list of items to clear up with the Lord and with other people, there's no need to be weighed down by undefined guilt. Why? Because the Holy Spirit who indwells us will clearly pinpoint the sins we've committed.

'Satan accuses but the Spirit convicts.' If you feel a vague sense of guilt but can't put your finger on a particular sin, that guilt probably is not from the Lord. Ask, 'God, is this sense of guilt from You? If so, please make clear what I've done wrong.' The Holy Spirit doesn't accuse us, condemn us or lay a cloud of guilt and depression over us. If we spend time quietly before the Lord, He will convict us of the specific sins we have committed.

Taking time to listen to the Lord and write down our sins is a crucial first step toward radical renewal. We're suddenly at a point of crisis. We have to make a choice. Proverbs 28:13 says,

'He who conceals his transgressions will not prosper, but he who confesses and forsakes them will obtain mercy' (RSV). We can choose to cover up our sins and reap the consequences. Or we can confess them and allow God to do a good work in our soul.

I urge you to do business with God without delay. In His presence, confess every sin the Holy Spirit brings to mind. You don't have to dredge up old sins that already have been forgiven. But ask the Lord to 'Cleanse me from secret faults' (Psalm 19:12 NKJV).

Are you willing to do it? Are you ready? I hope so. Even if you've asked God to search your heart before, ask Him now again. Write out your list, and then we'll consider what to do with it in the next chapter.

To Ponder

1. 'There is only one thing that can keep you and me from enjoying the Christian life to the fullest possible extent.' What is it? Have you seen its effects in your own life?

2. 'Unless we undergo God's divine surgery, sin will grow ever more malignant within our souls.' If we don't deal with unconfessed sin in our lives, what are some possible consequences? How can we become more sensitive to sin?

3. 'The secret of ongoing, continuous renewal is brokenness and repentance.' What needs to be scheduled into your life for that to happen?

4. 'Unbelief may be the most serious and devastating sin of all.' What fosters unbelief in our hearts? How can we protect ourselves from it?

5. 'Since our culture has made materialism almost a religion, it's extremely easy to become resentful.' How should we respond if we begin to feel resentful toward others who have things we don't have? What if we sense others feel resentful toward us?

6. 'We all have at least one recurring sin, a sin that keeps tripping us up.' What do you think may be your recurring

sin? How long has it been a problem? How do you deal with it?

7. 'God wants us to deal radically and ruthlessly with sin.' Why is God so concerned about sin in our lives? What are some of the consequences of unconfessed sin?

To Pursue

1. In this chapter, I've mentioned forty-three different sins that can keep us from enjoying the Christian life. This list of sins isn't exhaustive by any means, but take a minute or two to review it. Do you sense the Holy Spirit pricking your conscience in any of these areas?

absorbed with self	losing one's temper
adultery	lust
bad debt	lying
bitterness	moral indifference
broken friendship	neglect of the Lord's Supper
carelessness	petty complaining
cheating	pornography
covetousness	prayerlessness
demandingness	pride
disloyalty	property damage
divisiveness	recurring sin
envy	resentment
giving neglected	self-righteousness
gossip	sexual impurity
greed	strained family relationship
homosexual behaviour	substance abuse
impatience	thanklessness
independence	theft
jealousy	unbelief
lack of commitment to church	unhappiness
laziness	worry

2. Turn in your Bible to Psalm 19:2 and 139:23–24. Meditate on these verses and then use them to ask the Holy Spirit to search your heart and pinpoint specific sins.

3. After praying, take out your notebook and a pen. On the top left-hand side of one page write: 'Things I must get right with God this week.' Then list any known sins you need to confess to the Lord. Allow Him to examine every area of your life.

4. Then on the top right-hand side of the same page write: 'Things I must clear up with other people.' List the names of people you've sinned against, and a brief description of what you need to do to make things right.

5. If possible, immediately proceed to the next chapter and take the steps outlined there.

CHAPTER 5

THE CLEANSED LIFE

The Lord won't force us to admit we have been
contaminated as we've walked through this
world. But He says, 'If I don't wash you, you
can have no part with Me....'

As has happened in many cities, the skyline where I live in Portland has changed dramatically during the last decade or two. One of the most prominent new features is the Oregon Convention Center with its twin towers stretching 260 feet into the air above the massive complex.

Shortly before the new convention centre was completed this last year, however, the impressive looking jade-green glass towers suddenly posed a problem that threatened to delay the scheduled completion of the $90 million project.

Apparently back in the design stages, no one had stopped long enough to ask 'How is anyone going to ever clean those towers?' It wasn't until construction was well under way that someone recognized the problem. Standard window washing systems couldn't be used to clean the twin spires, so a Los Angeles-based engineering firm was hired to figure out a way to keep them from becoming permanently dirty and dis-coloured.

Thankfully, God thought about the problem of cleaning our hearts long before He created Adam and Eve. And He knew exactly what He was going to do to cleanse us thoroughly, even though the drama of redemption wasn't played out in human history for several thousand years.

It's the night before Jesus' crucifixion. Jesus knows that Judas has already betrayed Him. He knows what's going to happen during the next few agonizing hours. Yet during the evening meal something startling takes place. And in this event, we find the remedy for our sin.

'It was just before the Passover Feast. Jesus knew that the time had come for him to leave this world and go to the Father. Having loved his own who were in the world, he now showed them the full extent of his love.

The evening meal was being served, and the devil had already prompted Judas Iscariot, son of Simon, to betray Jesus. Jesus knew that the Father had put all things under his power, and that he had come from God and was returning to God; so he got up from the meal, took off his outer clothing, and wrapped a towel around his waist. After that, he poured water into a basin and began to wash his disciples' feet, drying them with the towel that was wrapped around him.

He came to Simon Peter, who said to him, "Lord, are you going to wash my feet?"

Jesus replied, "You do not realize now what I am doing, but later you will understand."

"No," said Peter, "you shall never wash my feet."

Jesus answered, "Unless I wash you, you have no part with me."

"Then, Lord," Simon Peter replied, "not just my feet but my hands and my head as well."

Jesus answered, "A person who has had a bath needs only to wash his feet; his whole body is clean. And you are clean, though not every one of you." For he knew who was going to betray him, and that was why he said not every one was clean.

When he had finished washing their feet, he put on his clothes and returned to his place. "Do you understand what I have done for you?" he asked them. "You call me 'Teacher' and 'Lord,' and rightly so, for that is what I am. Now that I, your Lord and Teacher, have washed your feet, you also should wash one another's feet. I have set you an example that you should do as I have done for you. I tell you the truth, no servant is greater than his master, nor is a messenger greater than the one who sent him. Now that you know these things, you will be blessed if you do them." ' (John 13:1–17)

Acknowledging Our Defilement

In New Testament times, people ate an evening meal while reclining on a couch or cushions on the floor around a low table. Before sitting down, however, everybody removed their sandals. Naturally, it wasn't very pleasant for others if you had dirty feet.

The guests may have taken a bath right before coming. But then they had to walk along dusty and dirty roads. Most streets were filled with a wide assortment of people and animals. Often city streets were littered with garbage and refuse. Their feet were inevitably dirty by the time they arrived at their destination. So the host normally had a servant or slave at the door to wash the feet of each guest and dry them with a towel. It was a disagreeable job, but it had to be done. Then the guests would walk into the dining area, visit with the host and enjoy a pleasant meal together.

On this particular occasion, however, Jesus and His disciples were borrowing a room to eat their final Passover meal together. They had no servants, and none of the disciples had thought about bringing a basin, towel, and pitcher of water to wash everyone else's feet. Only Jesus thought about it, because He 'did not come to be served, but to serve, and to give his life as a ransom for many' (Mark 10:45).

Try to picture this scene. Even though He knows His death is imminent, Jesus does the work of a slave. The Master Himself, the Son of God, the Creator of heaven and earth, got on His knees. The disciples should have washed His feet, but Jesus knelt and washed the feet of one of His disciples, then dried them with the towel He had wrapped around His waist. He then knelt by another disciple and washed his feet. Jesus kept going around the room until He reached Peter.

Suddenly the whole scene focuses on this one apostle. Peter

was one of the Lord's most prominent disciples. Whenever Jesus healed someone away from the crowds, Peter was there. When Jesus invited His closest disciples to witness His transfiguration, Peter was right there, too. Peter stood out among the disciples. He was a leader with a tremendous zeal for the Lord. As a spokesman for the group, he was the first to declare his belief in Jesus as the Messiah, the Christ, the unique Son of God. But Peter was also fallible. He tended to be rash, and his impulsive statements got him into trouble more than once.

When Jesus knelt to wash Peter's feet, Peter couldn't contain himself. 'What? Are You going to wash my feet?' The other disciples were paralysed, astonished that their Master would take the place of a slave. But Peter, with his big mouth, wouldn't let Jesus do it. The atmosphere in the upper room must have become electric at this point.

Now everyone in that upper room had come in with defiled and dirty feet. Just walking half a mile down the dusty, dirty streets of Jerusalem would have contaminated them. It didn't matter how recently they'd had a bath. Everyone had polluted feet. Everyone needed to have his feet cleansed.

Similarly, you and I often become defiled as we walk through this world. Even if we're trying to please God in everything we do and say, we still hear things we don't want to hear. We see things we didn't intend to see. We're defiled just going to the supermarket and coming straight home.

Many Christians work in offices or factories with men and women whose language and stories colour our thinking. It doesn't matter if we read Scripture, memorize key verses, spend time in prayer and sing choruses of praise to the Lord before going to work each day. Our mind is still polluted by the filth we hear.

Or maybe you work with people who dress handsomely or suggestively and who make passes at fellow employees and customers. You can't be around them long before you get polluted.

If we want to experience radical renewal, we need to be

honest enough to admit, 'Lord Jesus, I've been defiled as I've walked through this fallen world. I want to sit at the table of fellowship with You and with my brothers and sisters in Christ. But there's no way I want to sit there with dirty, polluted feet.'

That's the picture I see in the upper room. The disciples had arrived with dirty feet, so the Lord humbled Himself and washed their feet. The disciples were humble enough to let Jesus do it. Then Peter exposes his defiant heart.

Recognizing Our Defiance

Peter's dusty feet symbolized a deeper problem, only he wouldn't admit it. At first it sounds like Peter was being humble. But if you listen again, you can almost hear the pride and arrogance when Peter says, 'You will never wash my feet, Lord.'

What a contradiction! Peter wasn't talking to one of the other disciples. He was talking to Jesus Christ, the Messiah, the Saviour, the King of kings and Lord of lords.

But Peter's defiance didn't catch Jesus off guard. Jesus quietly and patiently and lovingly gave Peter the shock treatment. 'All right, Peter. You don't want Me to wash your feet? Fine. But if I don't wash your feet, you can have no part with Me.'

The Lord does the same thing with us. He won't force us to admit we've been contaminated by the world. He won't make us humbly pray, 'Master, wash me. I desperately need it.' Because He doesn't do that, we might think we're getting away with something. We could put up a front and pretend we're okay the way we are. But in our hearts the Lord is saying, 'You can have no part with Me.' No part in service. No part in worship. No part in fellowship. Oh, we can go to church and sing the songs and raise our hands. But the Lord still says, 'If I don't wash you, you can't have any part with Me.'

That's where an incredible number of Christians are stuck

today. Older men and women, even pastors and their spouses, have never progressed beyond this point—they've never been thoroughly cleansed from sin. They've never begun to experience God's renewal in their lives.

It's hard to think someone could be a child of God yet have a miserable, frustrated life. But it's true because of sin in his or her heart. Again and again the Lord has said, 'Please let Me wash your feet,' but the person keeps saying no. So the Lord responds, 'Well, then, you can't have any part with Me.'

The Lord uses strong words to slay Peter's pride. If Peter didn't permit the Lord to cleanse him from daily defilement, from the impurities of mind, heart and soul that accrued as he went through the world, he could have no part in fellowship with Christ. His words are meant for you and me, too. You may be a pastor. You may be an executive or professional. You may be a university professor or student. You may be a young person. But whatever your situation in life, if you're a Christian, then Jesus is saying to you, and saying to me, 'Let Me wash your feet. If I don't, you can have no part with Me.'

We can't pretend to walk in the light with God if we have polluted ourselves. Without that cleansing on a regular basis, we're still a child of God but we have no fellowship, no joy, no power. We're incapable of serving the living God (Hebrews 9:14). He can't use us.

Just as people in the first century had to wash their feet repeatedly, we too must have our spiritual feet washed day after day. Otherwise, we lose God's blessing on our life and ministry. You may be a missionary. Great! I love missionaries; my dad is in heaven because British missionaries brought the Gospel to our family. But are your feet washed? I may be gifted of God to win people to Jesus Christ. But if I start fooling around in my heart, why should God keep using me?

The Bible says that we who are teachers will be judged more strictly (James 3:1). We who lead and serve the Body of Christ have a double responsibility to walk in holiness. The holier we are, the more usable we are. So if you and I want to be used of God, if we want to have a part with Jesus, He says, 'Let Me wash your feet.'

God is a God of love. That's why He's at our feet, ready to wash them. But God is also just, and the two go together. You can't separate God's love from His justice. Therefore, it's ridiculous to think we can sin all we want 'and the God of love is going to have to forgive me'. What makes us think we're going to get away with that attitude?

The New Testament commands us not to play games with God. 'Do not be deceived. God cannot be mocked. A man reaps what he sows. The one who sows to please his sinful nature, from that nature will reap destruction; the one who sows to please the Spirit, from the Spirit will reap eternal life' (Galatians 6:7–8).

As far as you know, is everything right between you and your heavenly Father? Is everything clear between you and others? In other words, do you have clean feet?

Admitting Our Desperation

When Jesus gave Peter the shock treatment, he finally woke up to his desperate condition and cried out, 'Master, not my feet only! Wash my hands, wash my head. Pour it on. Do the whole job.'

Peter may have had a big mouth, but he had a quick brain and a good heart. To have no part with Jesus seemed intolerable to him. So Peter said, in essence, 'Lord, please don't toss me on the sidelines. Don't put me on the shelf. Don't file me away.' That was horrifying to Peter. And it's horrifying to imagine it happening to us, too. But if we refuse to be cleansed day by day, we will end up on the grandstands watching the game but never playing. We'll be on the bookshelf but never read. We'll be filed away like some old forgotten memo and never seen or used again. What an awful thought!

How does the Lord respond to Peter? 'Don't go overboard now, Peter. Listen, man, you've already had a spiritual shower the day you trusted in Me. He who is bathed needs only to wash his feet.'

And that's true in our lives, too. When we became Christians, all our sins were forgiven. We were washed in the blood of Christ. We've had a spiritual bath that the Bible calls salvation. But as we walk through this world, our feet become defiled. Sometimes we even become defiant, deliberately stepping into a mess by disobeying the Lord. Therefore, we need to sit humbly as Jesus, kneeling on the floor beside us, washes our feet. The Master is here, calling for you. He's kneeling at your feet, saying, 'Take off your shoes. You've picked up some of the dirt of this world. Let Me wash you now.'

The Lord can wash us because when He hung on the cross He took all our defilement and defiance on Himself. 'He himself bore our sins in his body on the tree, so that we might die to sins and live for righteousness; by his wounds you have been healed' (1 Peter 2:24). 'Christ died for sins once for all, the righteous for the unrighteous, to bring you to God' (3:18).

Have you lost the joy of the Lord? Have you lost your power? Have you lost your assurance? Come and get it. Don't wait another day. Go to the Lord and say, 'Master, You've seen my list of sins. You know everything I've done. Please wash me, cleanse me, purify me. I want to love You and serve You with all my heart again.'

Do that and you can claim this wonderful promise from God's Word: 'If we walk in the light, as he [God] is in the light, we have fellowship with one another, and the blood of Jesus, his Son, cleanses us from all sin' (1 John 1:7).

You and I need to ask, 'What have I done to hurt the Lord and His people?' Let us humbly confess our sins before the Lord and ask Him to wash us. Then let's go and clear up things with the person we've hurt or offended.

Don't say, 'I've already had my feet washed by the Master. I don't have to apologize to anyone.' If you and I are broken about our sin, we will clear the decks with other people. We will pay back what we've stolen. We'll be completely washed and freed from guilt.

What does the Bible say? 'If we confess our sins, he [God] is faithful and just and will forgive us our sins and purify us from all unrighteousness' (1 John 1:9). Not just from the little sins, but from all unrighteousness. What a word of forgiveness to claim!

You may be thinking, 'But Luis, I've committed a big sin. I mean, one of the big ones. Will God cleanse me from that?' Yes, if we confess our sins.

Now what is confession? Confession is simply stating what you've done. If a crook were confessing a crime he committed, he would tell the policeman or judge, 'Yes, I stole the goods. Yes, I pulled the trigger. Yes, I jumped the light and smashed into the old lady's car. I did it.' That's confession. If you begin to say, 'Well, you have to understand. I was playing with the gun...,' that's making excuses or lying outright.

Biblical confession means telling the Lord what you know you've done wrong, even if you've confessed that same sin many times before and you're ashamed to have to bring it up once more. Confession means admitting your recurring sins and acts of defiance. It even means saying, 'Lord, there may be some secret sins I'm not aware of yet.' The Lord will gladly wash you and eventually point out those hidden sins, too.

The first step toward radical renewal, as we saw in the last chapter, is to acknowledge our sins. That's confession. Perhaps you wrote down only one or two things. Maybe you have quite a lengthy list.

Now let's take the second step. Across your paper, write the words of three verses. First, 1 John 1:7: 'The blood of Jesus cleanses me from all sin.' Second, claim the Lord's promise in 1 John 1:9 and write, 'God forgives my sins and purifies me from all unrighteousness.' Third, personalize Hebrews 10:17 and write, 'My sins and lawless acts God will remember no more.'

Have you written those verses across your list? I've done this and I urge you to do it, too. Then if it expresses what's on your heart, I invite you to pray this prayer of confession and cleansing to the Lord:

'Lord, it's hard to believe that You would be at my feet, but there You are. Please wash me. It's obvious from my list that I've sinned against You. I've done things I shouldn't have done. And I have left undone things I should have done. I am unworthy of Your forgiveness. But thank You for Your blood, which cleanses me from all sin and unrighteousness. Now Lord, help me make restitution to those against whom I have sinned. Give me grace with the people I need to talk with; may they accept my apology. And help me to forgive those who have spoken evil against me or in some other way hurt me. Holy Spirit, help me never to think about those offences again. I want to be clear, free, joyful in You.'

Amen? When we confess our sins to the Lord, they're washed. They're cleansed. 'As far as the east is from the west, so far has he [God] removed our transgressions from us' (Psalm 103:12). The Lord has hurled 'all our iniquities into the depths of the sea' (Micah 7:19). As Corrie ten Boom used to say, 'The Lord takes our sins and casts them to the bottom of the sea. Then He puts out a little sign that says, "No fishing allowed." ' The Lord doesn't remember our sins anymore, and He doesn't want us bringing them up again, either.

Therefore, I urge you to look at your list and take care of anything you need to clear up with someone else. Do it quickly, in person or over the phone if necessary.

I know this part isn't easy. Sometimes the hardest people to face are those in our immediate family. At one point when my kids were young I felt there was something between me and one of my twins, Keith. So I talked with him and asked, 'Keith, have I done anything that really hurt your feelings? Or have I ever promised you something and disappointed you?'

Instantly Keith said, 'Yes. Last Christmas you promised to give me a toy submachine gun and you never gave it to me.'

The fact is, I'd completely forgotten all about it. I probed further: 'Is there anything else I've done that wasn't right and I've never asked for your forgiveness?'

Again, instantly, Keith said 'Yes.'

'And what was that?'

'You remember when Stephen was born?' Of course I remembered that. We were living in Mexico City at the time. 'When Mom said you had to go to the hospital because Stephen was going to be born, you left us at home and took off in a hurry. Remember?' I did.

'Well, you took off, you left Mom at the hospital, and you forgot the suitcase with all the stuff.' I couldn't believe all the details he remembered! 'So you came back and you were real huffy. When you got here, the suitcase had been opened and everything was thrown all over the place. And you spanked me.' My heart sank.

'And you didn't do it?' I asked.

'No, I didn't.' I felt terrible. I hugged Keith and asked him to forgive me. There was an instant improvement in our relationship after that.

That went so well that I called in Keith's twin brother, Kevin. After all, maybe I'd hurt him, too. 'Have I ever done something wrong and never asked your forgiveness or promised you something and never fulfilled it?'

Without any hesitation, Kevin said, 'Yes.'

'What was it?'

'Last Christmas you promised us a toy submachine gun and you never bought it for us.' Kevin had no idea I'd just talked to Keith about the same thing. Naturally, I took my sons to the store that day and bought one.

The important thing wasn't the silly toy. I probably wasn't paying attention when I made that promise. I certainly shouldn't have made that promise lightly. But I did, and I had to clear the decks with my boys.

If you suspect there's something between you and someone else, add that person's name to your list and talk to him. Humbly ask if you've done something to hurt or disappoint him. And be prepared to ask for his forgiveness and make things right again.

I want to add a word of caution. Talk to one person at a time. Don't confess something you've done wrong to anyone other than the individual you've wronged. Dealing with such matters in a group setting can be damaging. Wait until you can talk privately.

It may take time, but clear the decks with each person you've hurt or offended. Then take your list and tear it up with thanksgiving and a song of praise to the Lord. Don't keep it around to remind you of your past sins. They're gone forever.

What a sense of forgiveness and relief! But the Lord doesn't stop there.

Washing One Another's Feet

Do you remember what Jesus said after He washed the disciples' feet? 'Now that I, your Lord and Teacher, have washed your feet, you also should wash one another's feet. I have set you an example that you should do as I have done for you.... Now that you know these things, you will be blessed if you do them' (John 13:14–17).

Jesus had just washed everyone's feet. No one needed his feet washed a second time, did he? But Jesus knew He would be crucified the next day. He knew He was going back to the Father. And He knew His disciples would need to be cleansed again soon. So He commanded His disciples (and that now includes you and me) to wash one another's feet.

How do we wash one another's feet? Naturally, we're not in a position to forgive sins, but God can use us in the process of cleansing. Like Jesus, we can minister to a brother or sister in Christ who has become dirty or defiled by the world.

How often have you asked someone 'How are you?' and he's said 'Oh, great,' but you knew that person didn't mean it? Instead of sitting down and gently encouraging that person to open up, we often resort to trivial chatter or simply walk away, don't we?

If we're serious about washing one another's feet, we become sensitive to the feelings of others. We pay attention to the verbal and non-verbal signals they give. We discard any judgemental thoughts and ask, 'Is something wrong? How are you feeling? Can I pray with you?'

Notice you don't stand up to wash somebody's feet, you kneel. Humility and servanthood are prerequisites to being used by God in this vital ministry. There's no need to come on strong or pretend we have all the answers. We come on our knees (if not physically, by our attitude) and say, 'If I can serve you, if I can be of any help, let me know.' By doing that, we can help unleash God's blessing in the lives of others.

One of my team members (I'll call him Greg) was directing a 'united' evangelistic campaign in a city where two prominent pastors had fought for years. Many non-Christians knew about the feud between this Presbyterian minister and a Baptist preacher. My associate, Greg, tried to encourage them to patch up their differences, but it was no use.

For the sake of the Gospel, Greg decided to call these two pastors together and wash their feet. He invited both pastors to his home for lunch, but he didn't tell either gentleman that the other pastor was also invited. He scheduled the Baptist pastor to arrive half an hour earlier than the Presbyterian.

At lunch time the Baptist pastor arrived and chatted with Greg while his wife finished preparing lunch. Half an hour later the Presbyterian minister arrived. Both pastors suddenly stiffened. Greg was scared, but he invited these two men to sit down and quickly got to the point.

'I know you must be shocked and perhaps even upset that I've brought you together like this,' Greg said. Then he poured out his heart for these two older ministers. 'It's my responsibility to bring the Body of Christ together for the upcoming evangelistic campaign, but it isn't happening. And it's because you two men have been fighting. All the Christians know about it. Even many of the unconverted know you don't love one another, that you've had this bitter resentment against each other. You're hurting the Body of Christ and the testimony of the Gospel.

'So I feel we shouldn't have lunch today until you ask each other's forgiveness. I'm here to be of any help I can. I realize

I'm young, but nobody else in this city would do it. So before the Lord—if you will forgive me—I must be the person to do it.'

Both pastors broke down and confessed how they had sinned against each other, harboured resentment in their hearts, and hurt their testimony in that city. Together on their knees they asked for the Lord's forgiveness. And a tremendous breakthrough occurred.

People quickly learned about the reconciliation of these two pastors. The Baptist pastor, instead of marrying his son and future daughter-in-law in his own church, went over to the Presbyterian church and the two pastors performed the wedding ceremony together. As a result, the churches in that city united and we had a tremendous evangelistic campaign, with many making first-time decisions for Christ and several churches planted as a result. It was a thrilling crusade, but what would have happened if no one had obeyed the Lord's command, humbled himself, and in love washed the feet of those two pastors?

It takes a great measure of love to wash someone's feet, doesn't it? Why else would anyone humbly exhort or rebuke or correct us? Proverbs 9:8 says, 'Rebuke a wise man and he will love you.' So why don't we wash one another's feet more often? Speaking about myself, I know I can be quite indifferent toward others. I think thoughts like, 'I don't want to meddle in that person's life. If I do, he might tell me off. She might hate me. They're going to accuse me of sticking my nose into other people's business.'

I believe we end up causing untold harm when we notice someone who is hurting or lacking peace but say nothing. It's obvious our brother or sister has dirty feet. Maybe he's even become defiant in his attitude toward the Lord. Something is wrong, but we ignore it. We don't want to get involved.

A friend of mine was a successful businessman, an elder in his church and an excellent lay preacher. One day while we were eating out I noticed that this friend was eying the waitresses. Most men will notice a nice looking woman. But there's a difference between that and looking eagerly with lust in your heart. It seemed to me, and to several others, that our friend was struggling with lust. But because he was a respected Christian leader, we didn't say anything. We were indifferent instead of doing what Scripture says and humbly washing his feet in love.

Looking back, I think our friend would have confessed his sin if we had washed his feet. Instead, one day, four years later, I received a phone call from a mutual friend. 'Luis, I've got bad news. Our friend's wife came over to the house last night, sobbing because she thinks he's having an affair with a secretary at the office.'

I couldn't believe the news. But a few days later, while I was checking in at the airport for a trip to Los Angeles, a man accidentally shoved two heavy suitcases against my knee. I turned and saw it was my friend. He was shocked to see me, but pretended nothing was wrong and quickly said, 'Well, Luis! Good to see you. How are you doing?'

Tagging along behind this guy was a young woman...not his wife. At first he tried to distance himself from her, but it was obvious. Besides, his luggage didn't look right for a business trip. 'Uh, Luis, uh, meet Suzie.... She's a secretary at my company....'

I wept in my heart because I felt all along that if we had been men of God, four years earlier we could have done something. I should have gone to this friend and said, 'Look, we're all tempted, but you don't have to let lust overcome you. Let's look at what God's Word says. Let's get on our knees and take this to the Lord.' But I was indifferent, and now it was too late. He was committing adultery.

Later on my friend was filled with remorse and regret for what he had done. He repented before the Lord, was reconciled to his wife, and restored to fellowship in his church. But the scars will always be there—the agony, the suspicion, and all the other pain that follows adultery.

Galatians 5:1 says that 'if someone is caught in a sin, you who are spiritual should restore him gently'. In Matthew

18:15–17, the Lord gives further instructions if church discipline is in order. And in both of his epistles to the Corinthians, Paul models how to make those instructions work. The goal? To see our fallen brother or sister restored to fellowship with God and with others.

Sin always separates. If we see someone who seems to be stepping back away from the Lord or a spouse or other believers, there's no time to pretend everything is okay. We need to get on our knees before the Lord and intercede for that person. We need to humble ourselves and admit we're tempted by sin, too. Then we need to go to our friend and gently say, 'Listen, can I help you? Is something wrong? I've noticed....'

It's easy to notice when something's wrong in a friend's life and still say nothing. I was speaking at a conference centre one summer. A seminary professor and his wife on furlough from Asia were there. During the week I chatted briefly with this professor and noticed how sad he looked. I felt the Holy Spirit saying, 'Talk to this professor. Find out what's the matter. Try to encourage him....'

But I was busy. There were lots of other people to meet. I let it go. Six months later I found out that while this professor was teaching at the seminary one day, his wife wrote a little note. He found it on the kitchen table after she had already boarded a plane back to the United States. Her note said: 'I'm sick and tired of your work at the seminary and all this missionary garbage. Don't come looking for me. I never want to see you again.'

That was it. The marriage was over. Again, I had disobeyed the Holy Spirit. At the time, it seemed ridiculous that a seminary professor needed me to talk to him. But I should have done it anyway. Maybe I could have helped. I know I thank the Lord for the men He used early in my ministry to confront me in love about my pride and cockiness and aggressiveness. They were godly men, men of integrity. They knew what it was to be washed by the Master. And so, even though it was tough, they took me aside and washed my feet.

We all need to be washed, don't we? We need the Lord's cleansing. And we need to wash each other's feet. This is a critical element of radical renewal. But there's more. After confession and cleansing comes consecration.

To Ponder

1. The Lord wants us to experience the joy of sins forgiven, the excitement that everything is cleansed and cleared in His eyes and the eyes of others. Have you experienced that joy and excitement? Why don't most Christians experience it more often?

2. We may have sin on our conscience. The remedy for that sin is to be washed by Jesus. How is Jesus the remedy for sin? What did He do? What do we have to do?

3. 'You and I often become defiled as we walk through this world. Even if we're trying to please God in everything we do and say, we still hear things we don't want to hear. We see things we didn't intend to see.' How have you been unintentionally contaminated by the world this week? What was your response? What did you do to get rid of that contamination?

4. 'Just as people in the first century had to wash their feet repeatedly, we too must have our spiritual feet washed day after day. Otherwise, we lose God's blessing on our life and ministry, too.' Do you agree or disagree? Why? Think of an example.

5. 'Jesus commanded His disciples (and that now includes you and me) to wash one another's feet.' What was Jesus' concern? How should we go about washing one another's feet?

6. 'By washing one another's feet, we can unleash God's blessing in our life and in the lives of others.' Have you ever washed someone else's feet spiritually? Has anyone ever washed your feet? What happened?

7. 'It's easy to notice when something's wrong in a friend's life and still say nothing.' Why are Christians sometimes

afraid to say anything to fellow Christians? What motivates us to do something? What attitude should we have?

To Pursue

1. Take out your notebook and prayerfully review the 'Things I must get right with God' section of the confession list you wrote out for chapter 4. If anything else comes to mind, write it down. Ask God to make you sensitive to any and all defilement and defiance.

2. Turn in your Bible to 1 John 1:7 and 1:9, then Hebrews 10:17. Underline these verses and meditate on them. Personalize each promise and claim it for yourself. Then write the words of these promises across your 'Things I must get right with God' list.

3. Quietly offer a prayer of confession and cleansing to the Lord. Ask Him to wash your feet of all sin and impurity. You may wish to use the prayer suggested on page 90.

4. Turn in your Bible to Psalm 103:12 and Micah 7:19. Underline, meditate on, personalize and claim these promises, too. You may want to memorize these two verses so you can recall them whenever Satan reminds you of a sin you've already confessed and had cleansed by Christ.

5. Now prayerfully review the 'Things I must clear up with other people' section of your confession list. If there is anything you need to add to the list, write it down. Ask God for decisiveness, wisdom and tact to make things right.

6. Schedule time to meet with each person you've hurt or offended. If someone lives in another city, call him or her this week. If restitution is necessary, arrange to begin repaying your debt as soon as possible.

7. When you've cleared up everything written down on your confession list, tear it up with thanksgiving and a song of praise to the Lord. Get rid of it so no one will ever see it.

8. Turn in your Bible to John 13:14–17. Thank God for His desire to use us to minister to one another. Ask God to use someone, perhaps an older Christian in your church, to

wash your feet this week. Pray for love and gratitude to accept that person's words of concern and correction.

9. Ask God to make you sensitive to the hurts and feelings of other Christians. Pray for humility and wisdom to know what to say, and how to help.

10. If the Lord has already brought someone to mind who seems to be struggling, intercede for that person. Then look for an opportunity to talk heart to heart sometime soon. With a servant's heart, gently say, 'Can I help? Is something wrong? I've noticed....' Ask the Holy Spirit to direct your conversation and use you, if needed, to wash that person's feet.

CHAPTER 6

THE CONSECRATED LIFE

The next essential step toward radical renewal is
consecration. After salvation, it's the second
biggest decision God asks us to make....

A few summers ago two Britons ran 2,027 miles over the fourteen highest mountains in the world. Try that yourself and plan on climbing a whopping 290,000 feet traversing sixty-four mountain passes. The Himalayas furnish some pretty gruelling terrain, indeed.

Brothers Richard and Adrian Crane are reported to have run the length of the Himalayas in a record 101 days, all in hopes of raising money for a British charity. As it turned out, they suffered heat exhaustion, dysentery, heel blisters, torn nails, bruises and bleeding feet—plus one nasty gash to the head from a rock fall—to raise all of $10,700 by journey's end. That works out to less than two cents per thousand steps they pounded out. One hopes a few more donations have come in since!

Imagine trying to accomplish such a mega marathon feat. Especially if, like the Crane brothers, you had spent only two weekends running through the countryside before flying off to Darjeeling, India, to start your Himalayan trek.

The Cranes said their main training was mental, not physical. You know, 'Put your mind to it, and you can do anything.' While that doesn't always prove to be true, we all have a mind for something, whether it's music, money, power, sports, respectability, social status, a happy home or a comfortable life. Everybody's dedicated to something.

At some point, however, either at our conversion or sometime later, we all have to answer the question, Will I dedicate my life to Jesus Christ? Will I make everything else secondary and live for Him? Will I seek first the kingdom of God and His righteousness? Is it true for me that 'to live is Christ'?

Many Christians think they've dedicated their lives to the Lord, but they haven't given up the rights to certain areas of their lives. They haven't dealt with certain sins. They've gone only three-quarters of the way up Calvary's hill, but stopped short of the cross.

Perhaps no other incident in the life and ministry of Jesus Christ illustrates the radical call to consecration better than when the rich young ruler came running up to Jesus. From a human point of view, this man had it made. He had his youth. He had inherited immense wealth. He had a prominent social standing. He was religious. He had kept all the commands 'since I was a boy', he told Jesus.

But Jesus knew something the young man didn't. He put his finger on the young man's wealth. 'One thing you lack,' Jesus told him. 'Go, sell everything you have and give to the poor, and you will have treasure in heaven. Then come, follow me' (Mark 10:21).

The rich young ruler was staggered by Jesus' words. The disciples were staggered, too. And many Christians today still find Jesus' words hard to believe. 'Go, sell, give, come and follow.' What did He mean?

The rich young ruler never found out. He walked away, despondent over Jesus' words. What a pity he didn't wait three minutes to hear the Lord say, 'I tell you the truth, no one who has left home or brothers or sisters or mother or father or children or fields for me and the gospel will fail to receive a hundred times as much in this present age (homes, brothers, sisters, mothers, children and fields—and with them, persecutions) and in the age to come, eternal life' (Mark 10:29–30).

The young man walked away too quickly. If he had stayed just a few more minutes he would have realized that the Lord was asking for ownership, not demanding possession. I believe the Lord was going to tell him, 'Give it to Me, but don't worry. You'll get more than enough back.' If he had just asked, 'Lord, what am I going to do if you take my land? How am I going to live?' The Lord would have said, 'Don't worry. I'll give you a hundred times as much. I just want you to understand that I have a right to ask for any and all of it.'

What does God want with all our stuff? He owns the cattle on a thousand hills. That's not what He is after. He's addressing a bigger issue—the issue of consecration. Are we willing to surrender the rights to everything we own or wish we had? Are we willing to surrender our ambitions and dreams? That's the bottom line of consecration.

As the cross implies, consecration involves immense cost and sacrifice. Jesus said, 'If anyone comes to me and does not hate his father and mother, his wife and children, his brothers and sisters—yes, even his own life—he cannot be my disciple. And anyone who does not carry his cross and follow me cannot be my disciple' (Luke 14:25–27).

Those are strong words. Jesus isn't speaking about a flippant or light-hearted decision. He's talking about radical commitment. No wonder He went on to warn about counting the cost. If you start building a skyscraper but run out of money before it's finished, you end up looking like a fool. Counting the cost is important in the everyday affairs of life; how much more so when it comes to consecration.

When Jesus calls us to consecrate our lives, He's asking for a loyalty and love next to which all other loyalties pale into insignificance and all other loves appear to be hatred. The Lord is asking for total sacrifice, maximum surrender, the end of 'me' and 'my rights'.

Surrendering Our Rights

At a luncheon in a certain city a respected millionaire got up to testify that 'I owe it all to the Lord.' He then shared his secret. 'When I was a young fellow, a call was made for me to surrender all. Young as I was, and poor as I was, everything I had I surrendered to Christ. I didn't have much money, but I put it on the table, along with all my possessions, and said, "Christ, I give everything back to you." And it was after that that God began to bless me and now I'm a wealthy man.'

At that point, a voice from the back of the room shouted, 'I challenge you to do it again.'

Ever wonder why most of the people who respond to the call of a preacher to surrender 'all' are young? They don't have that much to surrender—three T-shirts, two pairs of jeans, and their dad's car keys. But when you get to middle age and own a house and two cars and a condo on the beach, it's a different story.

Surrender is a fundamental aspect of consecration, but today we want very little of it. Protecting our rights is much more important. The idea of giving up any rights cuts directly across our cultural bent.

We feel it's our inalienable right to be served. 'Submit to my husband? Who are you kidding? I'm not serving him. He'd better serve me or else I'm serving notice that I might just walk out on this family.'

Dr. James Dobson once asked me about this area of rights. We were talking about the pressures of travelling on family life, so I explained that I made it a point to spend as much time with the family as possible when home.

But I had to admit that I had been less than perfect. In fact, I used to come home and play golf with my pastor, shoot baskets with some friends, or go play tennis with a buddy. Then I realized, This is insane. Here I was travelling half the time and claiming I can't wait to get home. Then when I got home, I went out with my buddies.

Of course, I could argue that I needed the relaxation, I needed time for myself, that my friends were important, too.

But that evaded the issue. My family came first. In obedience to Christ, I gave up the right to spend my free time with friends. It wasn't easy, but it was crucial. Not that I was paying any big price, of course. I don't consider anything we do for Christ as paying a price. He paid the price, we don't. He owns us, not the other way around. But we often rebel against the idea of His Lordship over every area of our life.

Perhaps the hardest thing the Lord calls some of us to do is surrender the right to have our children near us. It's easy to get excited when a young man or woman goes forward at a mission conference pledging to become a full-time missionary overseas—unless it's your own child.

Some years ago I was invited to speak at the closing service at one of Multnomah School of the Bible's annual missions conferences. Afterward the president of the college, Dr. Ted Bradley, was standing in the lobby crying. 'It was moving to see your daughter dedicate her life to missionary service, wasn't it?' I asked.

'Actually, it's quite painful,' Dr. Bradley confided. 'I'm happy that she's going, Luis, and I know that I should be happy. But I keep thinking, "What if she dies in Africa?" It could happen. Or what if I die before she comes back?' And, as it turns out, he did.

Offering Our Body as a Living Sacrifice

It's never been easy to surrender our rights, take up our cross and follow Christ. Chuck Colson says, 'The idea of losing our lives for his sake, as Christ tells his disciples to do, is not any more popular today, in our obsessively materialistic society, than it was to the rich young ruler.'

By its very nature, biblical consecration is anything but a trendy, fashionable thing to do. It's much too costly, too life-threatening, too physical. You see this in the life of the apostle Paul. While in a Roman prison, with the threat of execution over his head, Paul could say, 'I eagerly expect and hope that I will in no way be ashamed, but will have sufficient courage so that now as always Christ will be exalted in my body, whether by life or by death' (Philippians 1:20).

Paul goes on to say, 'For to me, to live is Christ and to die is gain. If I am to go on living in the body, this will mean fruitful labor for me. Yet what shall I choose? I do not know! I am torn between the two: I desire to depart and be with Christ, which is better by far; but it is more necessary for you that I remain in the body' (Philippians 1:21–24).

Did you notice how often Paul talks in this brief passage about his 'body'? As far as he knew, his heart was right with God. But Paul talks here about exalting Christ 'in my body'. No doubt he knew he could have his head cut off, he could be fed to the lions, or he could be stoned to death at the whim of some corrupt or conniving politician. The Romans had a whole repertoire of miserable ways to die.

But Paul says, 'I don't know what to choose—life or death.' Which would you choose? Paul honestly struggled whether to accept martyrdom or earnestly pray for release from prison. He had consecrated his body to God.

In 1 Corinthians 6, Paul talks about the body again. There he explains the importance of fleeing from sexual immorality, whether adultery or homosexuality or prostitution. Why? Because 'All other sins a man commits are outside his body, but he who sins sexually sins against his own body' (6:18).

Why is Paul so concerned about the body? He answers that question by saying, 'Do you not know that your body is the temple of the Holy Spirit, who is in you, whom you have received from God? You are not your own; you were bought with a price' (6:19–20a). That price was the very blood of Jesus Christ, our Saviour. 'Therefore honour God with your body' (6:20b). Again, Paul has consecration in mind.

That's not all Paul has to say about the body. He talks about it again in Romans 12:1–2, a famous passage that many of us have memorized: 'Therefore, I urge you, brothers, in view of God's mercy, to offer your bodies as living sacrifices, holy and pleasing to God—which is your spiritual worship. Do not conform any longer to the pattern of this world, but be transformed by the renewing of your mind. Then you will be able to test and approve what God's will is—his good, pleasing and perfect will.'

When Paul says, 'I urge you,' he isn't making a suggestion or proposal. The Holy Spirit is presenting an urgent message through the mouth of Paul. So what is the message? 'Offer your bodies as living sacrifices, holy and pleasing to God— which is your spiritual worship.' This time our 'bodies' are connected with 'spiritual worship.' Paul says it's a decision every one of us has to make.

You can't divorce decisions from the Christian life. Some psychologists say one of the primary causes of emotional breakdowns is irresponsibility—refusing to take responsibility for our actions. Decisions are important! Most people don't like making them, but following Jesus Christ requires certain specific, clear-cut decisions.

Have you presented your body as a living sacrifice to the Lord yet? This is so important because our body is a symbol of our whole personality. It's the most tangible and practical thing we can present to the Lord. The soul we can't see. The spirit we can't see. But we're very concerned about the body, and it's the one part of us we most often hold back from Him. But when we present our body to God, the soul and spirit quickly follow.

I tell you, presenting your body to God is a liberating step. It's a step I wish millions of Christians would take.

You may be thinking, 'Why all the fuss about the body? I mean, it's just going to die one of these days anyway. The body is the least important part of me. The soul and spirit are much more important.'

Let's evaluate that for a moment. Most of us spend far more time looking in the mirror at our body than we spend looking in God's Word at our soul and spirit. Our culture almost worships the body, but the soul and spirit seem a bit ethereal. When we get up in the morning, we don't want anyone to see us until we've fixed up how we look. We're desperate to protect ourselves from any negative attention.

Some people don't put it in words, but their private feeling is: 'I'm sure glad my soul and spirit are going to heaven when I die. But my body, well, I'll dedicate it to the Lord in about thirty years. You only live once. I need to give my body a chance to express itself awhile. I won't do it all, but you know....'

The Lord knows, all right. Our hearts are desperately wicked. I can verify that. And you're just like me. The only difference is the way our bodies look. But inside, we're all alike. I know you because I know me. I can talk openly because I know what goes on inside us all.

Someone has noted that 'The body is the last thing we surrender to God.' We give Him our spirit and say, 'Lord, save me.' We give Him our soul and say, 'Lord, keep me happy and balanced.' But the body is the last citadel we allow God to invade. Yet the Lord Jesus said, 'Whoever wants to save his life will lose it, but whoever loses his life for me and for the gospel will save it' (Mark 8:35).

Why do we try to cling to our bodies so desperately? In my case, I think it was a combination of biblical ignorance, spiritual blindness, ingrained self-centeredness and basic distrust of the goodness of God.

Really, all those reasons revolved around my stubborn refusal to say 'yes!' to the Lord and consecrate myself to Him. And as I explained in chapter 2, that's when my spiritual crisis began.

I believe God brings each Christian to this point of crisis. If we refuse to consecrate our lives to Him, He brings us back to this crisis point again and again. But there comes a time, I feel, when the Lord says, 'I will push you only so far,' if we're insistent on going our own way.

Not Holding Back Anything

Consecration is an act of the will. It's a personal crisis before the Lord with immense consequences. We can't hold back in any area. The Lord is saying, 'I want either all or nothing.' So until we give Him our body, we've given Him nothing at all.

But with consecration comes conflict. Remember, we're in the midst of spiritual warfare. Consecration is a direct threat to the world's dominion in our lives. The world won't go down without a fight. The moment we say, 'Lord Jesus, You asked for my body and here it is,' we're automatically saying no to worldly talk, worldly thought, worldly things.

The decision to consecrate ourselves to God is tough, especially for those who find themselves enchanted by the world. The funny thing is, the world doesn't care a thing about you and me.

When I was young I tried to please the world. I tried desperately to win the flattery of people around me. Thankfully, as I related earlier in this book, the Lord dealt with me and brought me to a point of crisis. I felt like God was saying, 'Luis, a few more weeks of this and you're finished.' I could see it coming. I'd been walking away from God for several years. I'd pushed things to the limit. That's when I got down on my knees and said, 'Lord, have mercy. I'll serve You and give my whole life to You.' Having made that simple yet profound decision, my life began to change radically.

If you're tired of catering to the world's latest fads, if you're weary of giving in to the lusts of the flesh, if you've had it trying to live like the devil, take this next step. Don't play games with God. Don't miss out on everything God still has in store for you. Consecrate your life to Him today. Don't let another hour go by.

Perhaps you made this decision years ago as a young man or young woman. You may have even gone forward at a special camp or church meeting. You began to enjoy the Christian life in a new way. But then later something happened. You gave in to sexual temptation. You married a non-Christian. You cheated in college or in a business deal. You did something but never made things right. You've never forgotten the matter, and you shouldn't forget it until you ask for forgiveness.

The fact is, you used to be happy in the Lord. But since that setback, you've had a huge spiritual parenthesis in your life. You've had no victory, no joy, no growth. If that's the case, why not consecrate your life anew? Say, 'Lord, I put myself back on Your altar again. I'm all Yours. Take my body. Fill my heart. I give myself to You.'

I make no apology about repeatedly urging you to consecrate your life to God, because the day I made this decision was a day of new beginnings for me. Is God speaking to your heart? My prayer is that the truths of God's Word, especially Romans 12:1–2, will move you to make this step. Offer your body as a living sacrifice, holy and pleasing to God. It's an act of worship. It's a rational decision of the will.

Consecration Involves Both a Crisis and a Process

This crisis of consecration leads to a process that continues for the rest of our lives. Consecration isn't a one-time decision that we never think about again. It doesn't permanently eliminate conflict in our soul.

The process of consecration involves continuous, ongoing obedience and submission to God. It means repeatedly surrendering our natural rights for the greater spiritual good. In a fallen world, Jesus had a right not to die, let alone be spat upon, cruelly mocked, and beaten unmercifully. Yet He didn't make use of those rights. He allowed Himself to be scourged and crucified for the greater good, in obedience to the Father's will.

Likewise, every time our will crosses God's revealed will, we make a decision. If we choose His revealed will over our own will, we're surrendering our rights. We're consecrating our lives.

This is what Scripture means when it speaks of the death of Jesus, of taking up the cross, of the grain of wheat falling into the ground and dying. Whenever I choose God's revealed will, it is death to my ego, death to my pride, death to my ambitions and dreams.

Every decision in life is another opportunity to say 'yes!' to God, to affirm His Lordship over my body, soul, and spirit. Each time I choose God's will over my will, I'm becoming more like Christ. I'm testing and approving His will, that which is good and acceptable and perfect.

This is what it means to live in triumph and victory. Suddenly, we're no longer faced with decisions like whether or not to marry a non-Christian, whether or not to cheat on an expense account, whether or not to flirt with someone we like. What could be a terrible struggle becomes a tremendous relief. The issue is settled. By gladly choosing God's will, we're free to move ahead with renewed strength and vigour. We're no longer playing games with God. We still face our enemies—the world, the flesh and the devil—but now we enjoy victory and walk in holy boldness as ambassadors for Christ.

Consecrating Your Life Today

It's not too late to come back to the living God and consecrate yourself to Him. Perhaps you'd like to join me in this prayer of dedication: 'Oh God, solemnly in Your presence I present my body as a living sacrifice, holy and pleasing to You. Take my body, as a symbol of all that I am. It's Yours. I can't wait to see what You're going to do in and through my life for the glory of Your name. Amen.'

This could be the most exciting moment of your life. You are now walking by faith with your eyes and ears wide open, in great expectation, wondering what God is going to do. You will have your ups and downs. You will have your moments of darkness. But when you make that commitment, it's amazing what can begin to happen.

If you've just consecrated your life to God, you've made the second biggest decision in the Christian life. But there's one more decision to make—one final key to radical renewal.

We're going to see how to experience Christ's resurrection power!

To Ponder

1. 'Consecration involves immense cost and sacrifice.' When Jesus calls us to consecrate our lives, what is He asking for? What does it reveal about our heart if we refuse to respond to His call? What are the consequences of saying no?

2. 'When Jesus calls us to consecrate our lives, He's asking for a loyalty and love next to which all other loyalties pale into insignificance and all other loves appear to be hatred.' What authority does Jesus have to call us to consecrate our lives to Him?

3. 'The idea of giving up any rights cuts directly across our cultural bent.' From the world's perspective, what rights seem to be the most important today? Whose rights seem most important? How does that perspective differ from God's?

4. 'Consecration means surrendering our natural rights for the greater spiritual good.' What rights have been important to you? Which seem to be the hardest to surrender to Christ? Why?

5. 'If we present our body to God, the soul and spirit quickly follow.' Why is God so concerned about the body? What makes us so reluctant to surrender our body to the Lord?

6. 'The decision to consecrate ourselves to God is tough, especially for those who find themselves enchanted by the world. The funny thing is, the world doesn't care a thing about you and me.' What makes the world seem so enchanting? What prompts many Christians to try to win the world's praise?

7. After consecrating ourselves to God, 'every decision in life is another opportunity to say "yes!" to God, to affirm His Lordship of our body, soul and spirit'. Think of a recent decision where you had to decide between God's will and

your own. What did you decide to do, and what were the consequences?

To Pursue

1. In your notebook, write a couple of paragraphs describing to what you've consecrated your life in the past.

2. Turn in your Bible to Luke 14:25–27 and Matthew 10:37–38. Count the cost of following Christ by listing in your notebook what you believe the Lord is asking you to give up so you will be consecrated completely to Him.

3. Now turn to Romans 12:1–2. Take a few minutes to read these verses several times. Then in your notebook rewrite the verses in your own words, as if God were speaking directly to you.

4. Quietly before the Lord pray a prayer of consecration to the Lord. If you've already made that decision in the past, but then had a spiritual parenthesis in your life, consecrate your life anew. You may wish to use the prayer suggested on page 110.

5. Record the date of your decision in your diary or journal. Or take a page in your notebook to document it. Then tell your pastor or another significant Christian friend about your decision. If there's an opportunity at your church, go forward to publicly demonstrate your new commitment to Christ.

CHAPTER 7

THE CHRIST-CENTERED LIFE

The potential of what Christ wants to do in us
and through us for His glory is incredible. But
how often we don't realize that potential.
It isn't that we aren't trying. Sometimes we're
trying incredibly hard to live the Christian life
and be a good witness. And that's the problem....

When I think of the power of God at work in someone's life, I often think of Gladys Aylward. She has been rightly called the most noted single woman missionary in the twentieth century. Her story has been told in a popular biography, a film starring Ingrid Bergman, and a BBC *This Is Your Life* feature.

To meet Gladys Aylward in her younger days, however, you would have wondered what all the fuss was about. Born into a working-class family, Gladys did poorly in school and began work as a maid at age fourteen. And she would have remained a maid for life if God hadn't intervened.

Well into her twenties, Gladys was won to the Lord by a pastor's wife who had a passion for the lost—whether they be rich or poor. After her conversion, Gladys' vision expanded far beyond the corner of London where she worked. She began dreaming of telling the lost about her Saviour, feeling distinctly called by God to go to China as a missionary. But the mission board to which she applied couldn't have been less enthusiastic.

That didn't matter to Gladys. Convinced that God was leading her to China, Gladys set out at age thirty by train across Europe and Asia. That she made it to China at all is a miracle. On one occasion, Gladys found herself in a deserted train stranded in Siberia—only a minute from where Russian and Chinese soldiers were at war.

Once in China, God allowed Gladys to undergo some harrowing experiences but used her to win many Chinese to Himself. She demonstrated courage and physical endurance where many a man would have wilted. The secret wasn't her background, education or missionary training. By all standards, she didn't measure up. But because her life was centered on the Lord alone, He was pleased to demonstrate His power through her.

God wants to show His power in and through each of us, too, whatever our circumstances and calling in life. What's the secret? Consecration is essential, but by itself isn't enough. Some people have dedicated and rededicated and super rededicated their lives to God. But they still feel anything but renewed. 'Where's the touch of God on my life?' they wonder. 'Why don't I feel His presence at work within me?'

Experiencing radical renewal means being 'filled to the measure of all the fullness of God' (Ephesians 3:19). To be renewed means to be completely, totally filled with God Himself. That should be the normal Christian life.

The potential of what Christ wants to do in us and through us for His glory is incredible. But how often we don't realize that potential. It's not that we aren't trying. Sometimes we're trying incredibly hard to live the Christian life and be a good witness. And that's the problem.

Zeal for God Isn't Enough

The greatest fact in all of history is that the Lord has chosen to come and indwell us. Think of it! Almighty God lives in us. This fact revolutionized my life when I understood it for the first time. I had already dedicated and rededicated my life to Christ probably a dozen times. But every time, I took off with great zeal and high expectations only to come crashing back down to 'reality'.

The problem was I was always trying zealously to sweat it

out for God. Always trying to be faithful, always trying to overcome temptation by sheer dedication, discipline, Bible study, and prayer. It was Luis and his friends trying and trying and trying to be faithful to the Lord.

We were honest. We were sincere. We were zealous. We tried about everything to win people to Christ—sharp looking tracts, evangelistic radio programmes, enthusiastic street meetings. Some would listen; others would ridicule. But we saw few trust Jesus Christ as Saviour. Then some of my closest friends fell away from the Lord. Not completely at first, but they cooled off. Eventually our all-Friday-night prayer meetings dried up, too.

Up to that time, I was quite self-confident and ego-centered. 'God, You really got Yourself a prize in me. I tell You, Lord, I'm going to be dedicated till death. If I have to die for the kingdom, I'll die.' In my little heart was a feeling that 'I'm going to show the world what a young man can do for God.' It was a sincere desire.

But 'reality' is you get exhausted trying to live for God in your own strength. It's futile. Even a zealous, dedicated, consecrated Christian cannot live for God. We can clench our teeth, tighten our fists, and grimly determine we're going to pray, read the Bible, study, witness and live for God alone. But after a while even the most zealous Christian will end up feeling, 'What's the use? I'm so tired and nothing's happening, anyway. I don't have what it takes to live the Christian life. I give up.'

God can hardly wait for us to admit we can't live the Christian life as He intended. Why? Because the only person who could ever live the Christian life was Christ Himself. Frankly, it's only when we're defeated, when we're flat on our face, when we're completely wiped out, that we're ready to discover the greatest truth of the Christian life.

It's futile trying to please God in our own strength. But, praise the Lord, He is pleased to live in us! This is the fact that changed my life: we're united with Christ, and He wants to manifest His resurrection life through you and me.

The apostle Paul said, 'I want to know Christ and the power of his resurrection and the fellowship of sharing in his sufferings, becoming like him in his death' (Philippians 3:10). However, we first have to be crucified with Christ before the power of His resurrection life can surge through us.

Most of us are so stubborn that it takes years before we die to self. We resist it with all our might. We fight and rebel against it. We say, 'What are You doing? God, are You trying to tell me I don't have what it takes?'

That's exactly what God is trying to tell us. 'You don't have what it takes to live for My glory. But I do,' says the Lord. 'And all My resources are yours.' Do you believe that?

The Heart of the New Testament

Even though most of us didn't understand it at the time, becoming a Christian is tantamount to being invaded. 'He who unites himself with the Lord is one with him in spirit' (1 Corinthians 6:17). It's no longer God up there, and you and me down here. We're no longer separated. We don't talk to God at a distance. We're one spirit now. God came down to take up residence within us.

In Revelation, Jesus says, 'Here I am! I stand at the door and knock. If anyone hears my voice and opens the door, I will come in and eat with him, and he with me' (3:20). Although this is a wonderful illustration to use when inviting someone to trust Jesus Christ, it's really a word to us as Christians.

Jesus is speaking about our heart. He says it has a door that can be opened only from the inside. He will never try to smash it open. He simply knocks. Only we can open the door and let Him in. The question is, will we?

'How do I open the door?' you ask. It's as if I were to go to your house tonight and knock on your front door. You look out the window and say, 'Oh, my goodness. It's Luis Palau.' You have to make a decision. 'What are we going to do? This guy talks too much. Shall we let him in or not?'

If you decide 'yes', all you have to do is open the door and say, 'Come in, Luis. Sit down. Take off your coat. What would you like to drink?' And I walk into your house.

That's what Jesus is saying to us. 'I stand at your door. I am knocking. Have you heard my call? Open the door,' he says, 'and I will come in and eat with you and you with me.' In other words, we will experience the reality of His presence in our life. And what a delight that is!

Do you really believe that God lives in you? Are you enjoying that reality? I'd like to challenge you to discover this truth in the Scriptures for yourself. Try underlining every verse you can find that speaks of God being one with us. You'll be amazed at all the references, especially in the Gospel of John and the epistles. This is what I consider to be the heart of the New Testament message.

Let me give you just a sample. In Matthew 1:23, Jesus is named 'Immanuel'—'God with us.' That's only the start. God is now in us, and wants to fill us completely.

Paul asks, 'Do you not know that your body is a temple of the Holy Spirit, who is in you, whom you have received from God?' (1 Corinthians 6:19). Whether your body is fat or skinny, tall or short—if you're a Christian, God dwells in you.

That's why the thought of sexual immorality should be so repulsive to a Christian. When we trusted Christ, our body became a sanctuary for God's Holy Spirit. Anything that would grieve Him should grieve us. To think that we would defile God's temple is horrifying. God no longer says, 'Take off your sandals—this is holy ground.' He says, 'Put off your old ways—you now are to be holy, just as I who indwell you am holy.'

To perceive this marvellous truth is to wonder, 'Oh Lord, why did it take me so long to understand that the secret of the Christian life, the central theme of the New Testament, is Christ living in me?'

People will object, 'But I thought the foundation of the message of the New Testament is the work of Jesus Christ on the cross.' It is. But why did Jesus go to the cross? Because He wants to fill us. He couldn't indwell us, however, until sin was cleansed. Sin couldn't be cleansed until His work was done on the cross. Therefore, the cross was a necessary preliminary for God's ultimate objective, which is to unite us with Himself forever.

Galatians 2:20 ties these two issues together. It says, 'I have been crucified with Christ and I no longer live, but Christ lives in me. The life I live in the body, I live by faith in the Son of God, who loved me and gave himself for me.'

Notice the twin truths of this verse. First, 'I have been crucified with Christ.' From God's perspective, we are dead to sin. Sin has nothing to do with us and we have nothing to do with it. From our perspective, we hate sin. We hate it in ourselves; we hate it in other people. We never want to touch it again. When we fall into it, we quickly confess our sins and step back into God's light. This is the attitude of crucifixion.

The second truth is, 'Christ lives in me.' This is the key to radical renewal. There are other concomitant facts and practices that must go along. Yet we experience God's renewal within us when you and I not only understand but also accept this truth—Christ literally lives in us!

It's not enough to be consecrated. There's a danger in looking back at the day when we took Romans 12:1–2 to heart and dedicated our lives to Jesus Christ. Yes, we need to know that at some point we put ourselves on the altar, so to speak. But victory doesn't come from looking back and rejoicing over that decision.

The Lord desires that we live today enjoying the fact, 'It's not I, but Christ who lives in me.' The resurrected life of Christ in me is a living truth, not an experience we had sometime in the past.

But so many Christians have not taken this last step. That's why you meet people who are consecrated but powerless. They've definitely made a commitment to Christ, perhaps at a camp, a conference or a special series of meetings in their church. They can show you the date of their consecration in the front leaf of their Bible. But they're powerless. They're depressed and can't seem to rise above their circumstances.

In Philippians 4:12, Paul talks about his circumstances and says, 'I know what it is to be in need, and I know what it is to have plenty. I have learned the secret of being content in any and every situation, whether well fed or hungry, whether living in plenty or in want.' Adverse circumstances didn't get him down.

The question is, 'Paul, how did you learn that? Where did you get that kind of ability?' Most of us don't handle poverty very well, or riches for that matter. How did Paul do it? His secret: 'I can do everything through him who gives me strength' (4:13). Christ was Paul's source of strength in every situation.

In Colossians 1:27, Paul speaks of 'the glorious riches of this mystery, which is Christ in you, the hope of glory'. This truth so thrilled Paul that he laboured—'struggling with all his energy, which so powerfully works in me'—to proclaim it throughout the Roman Empire. It wasn't Paul striving in his own energy. The key to his amazing influence was 'Christ living and working in me'.

Paul talks about this again in Colossians 2:9–10. In Christ 'the whole fulness of the deity dwells bodily, and you have come to fulness of life in him, who is the head of all rule and authority' (RSV).

If Christ is God, and He is, and if He indwells every believer, and He does, then all the fullness of God indwells us! Not because we're something, but because the One who is everything fills us!

Was this theme merely a hobby horse of Paul's, or the very heartbeat of our Saviour? Consider the Lord's High Priestly prayer in John 17. Fervently He prayed that all believers 'may be one, Father, just as you are in me and I am in you. May they also be in us so that the world may believe that you have sent me. I have given them the glory that you gave me, that they may be one as we are one: I in them and you in me. May they be brought to complete unity to let the world know that

you sent me and have loved them even as you have loved me'
(17:21-23). What an amazing prayer Jesus prayed for you and
me!

What temptation could you face that Jesus does not have
the power to overcome?

What need will I ever have that the living Lord Jesus cannot
meet?

What wisdom would we need that He cannot provide?

If this truth grips your heart, it will revolutionize your life.
Yet most of the Christians I meet know nothing of the fullness of God. They have never experienced the joy and power
and victory of the Christ-centered life. They haven't recognized that it's not enough to receive Jesus Christ (John 1:12),
to open the door of their heart to Him (Revelation 3:20).

The Lord doesn't want to simply take up residence in our
life. Sure, He indwells every believer. But He wants to fill
every fibre of our being! Do you remember what He said? 'I
am the vine; you are the branches. If a man remains in me and
I in him, he will bear much fruit; apart from me you can do
nothing' (John 15:5).

Have you ever looked at a grape vine? It's often almost
impossible to tell where the vine stops and the branches begin.
They're intricately connected to one another. They 'abide' in
each other. Working together, they produce much fruit.

Scripture isn't speaking symbolically or figuratively about
Christ's desire to 'abide' in us. As branches, we are entirely
connected with the true Vine. We're one spirit. Nothing can
separate us. He indwells us. We can do all things through
Christ, who wants us to bear much fruit for His Father's
glory. He wants to control and bless everything we think and
do and say.

Abiding in Christ is a fact we need to understand and act
upon day by day. It isn't a decision we make, 'I must abide
with Christ. I must become a fruitful branch.' Jesus said we're
already branches. We're joined to Him, and without Him, we
can do nothing.

The problem is many Christians don't understand the

Christ-centered life. When they understand it, they find it hard to believe. And when they believe it, they find it hard to know how to take hold of what Jesus has to offer and live it out day after day. But if they did, the Church would be a powerhouse!

Can you imagine millions of Christians who actually believed—as they drive to work and go about their tasks— that God indwells them? Christians who lived in 'conscious, constant communion' with Christ? Why, the power would be incredible. Even with the weaknesses we all have, the power would be tremendous.

It can happen. All the resources of Jesus Christ are entirely at our disposal. Because He indwells us, all that is Christ's is ours. Yet how little we draw from those infinite resources. That's why we have powerless Christians—fruitless, joyless, and defeated.

The Day Christ Took Over

No one can live the Christian life except Christ Himself. I'll never forget the look on the face of an older missionary in Colombia when this truth dawned on him. I'd been asked to speak to a group of missionaries at a conference, during my first year on the field. My theme was the indwelling Christ as our resource and power to serve.

Afterward, this old missionary gentleman invited me to go for a walk with him. With tears streaming down his face, he told me, 'Luis, I have been here on the field for over thirty years. Everybody thinks I'm a great pioneer missionary. Yes, I've planted a few churches because I've preached the Gospel. But my wife and I have never had joy. We've talked about it for hours. Why don't we enjoy the Christian life? Why is it such a chore? Why do we always seem to be struggling?

'Now I see why. I've worked for God as hard as I could, with every ounce of my being, but it's brought little but frustration. Until today, I don't think I have ever really known what it means to allow the risen Christ to do the living in me. Why didn't someone tell me about this before?' My heart went out to this man, a genuine servant of the Lord, but one who had little fruit in his life or ministry.

It wasn't until eight years after I'd consecrated my life to God that I understood that Jesus Christ literally lives in me, Luis Palau, and that He wants to fill me to all the fullness of God.

This fantastic truth doesn't sink in easily. Fortunately, I finally understood it when I was twenty-five years old. I'm glad I didn't have to wait until I was in my sixties or later to learn it. Oh, I had all the right information. I could show you outlines in my notebooks about the Christ-centered life written before that age. But this truth meant nothing to me experientially.

The final link occurred for me when I heard Major Ian Thomas speak at Multnomah School of the Bible. As I related in chapter 2, Major Thomas was speaking about Moses and the burning bush. Forty years before the incident, Moses had thought of himself as a highly trained, educated, experienced man. He probably felt a definite call from God to liberate His people. But Moses thought he could serve God in his own power—in the energy of the flesh. His plans backfired, and Moses ended up running for his life.

After forty years of fruitlessness, uselessness and despair, Moses noticed a burning bush and turned aside to take a closer look. In the burning bush, the Lord appeared to Moses. 'What was the Lord trying to teach Moses?' Thomas asked. Basically this: 'Moses, I don't need a pretty bush or an educated bush or an eloquent bush. Any old bush will do, as long as I am in the bush.'

I felt the Lord saying to me, 'Luis, this message is for you. You must make a decision.' And the decision is this: to let Christ control me from within. I was to learn the truth of these words: 'Not I, but Christ. He lives in me!'

This is the third big decision we have to make. The Bible teaches that if you want a fruitful life, if you want victory to overcome temptation, if you want power and authority, then it can't be you. It must be Christ!

That decision revolutionized my life. Many things still had to be worked out, but my biggest spiritual struggle was finally over. I preached many of the same messages I had preached before, only now I saw fruit. People were being converted. Now I experienced power. There was authority; there was victory; there was freedom; there was joy. I finally understood what Paul meant when he said, 'If anyone is in Christ, he is a new creation; the old has gone, the new has come!' (2 Corinthians 5:17). The Lord changed the way I thought, the way I felt about people, the whole way I went about life.

Too many Christians live the way I lived for too many years. They believe that if they pray enough, read enough, and work enough, they'll be victorious. It cannot be done. We cannot work or earn our own victories through any self-effort, any more than we could work for our salvation.

Perhaps this sounds too easy. You can't believe that you can rely on the power of the resurrected Christ rather than on self-control, where the struggle is almost unbearable.

Fullness Versus Fruitless Frustration

Let's face it. A lot that goes on in even the best circles is dead. We've learned the techniques of fund-raising, publicity, mobilizing people, putting on a show, making a video, marketing products. We've got the techniques. But where's the reality? If God put the whole lot to the test today, much of what we admire would go up in smoke. It's nothing more than evangelical dead wood, hay and stubble. It won't stand up in the fire.

The secret isn't seminary training. It's not being well dressed. It's not good looks or networking or money or dynamic programmes or know-how. All of those things may have their place. But unless we're depending on the indwelling Christ, it's all a waste of time.

Why didn't the burning bush turn to ashes as Moses

watched? Because it was the fire of God, not the fire of the flesh. The fire that isn't of God consumes people. That's why we have Christian workers who give up and burn out. We sympathize with them and pamper them and have psychological counselling for them. But why do they burn out? Because they don't serve in the fire of God, but in the imitation fire of the flesh.

I've been in Christian service thirty years, long enough to tell you by name the stories of dozens of people who had great potential for God. I've seen men who were tremendous expositors, preachers, teachers, and musicians who spiritually are on the bench today. Some committed gross sins, others just ran out of fire because they were using the gifts of God with the fire of the flesh.

I think of an evangelist we worked with in South America who wrote fantastic sermons. He would preach the Gospel in twenty-five minutes and make it so attractive that unbelievers could hardly wait to respond when he gave the invitation. I would have loved to have been his crusade director. But we soon discovered he was using the gifts of the Spirit with the fuel of the flesh. He had an attitude toward money that was unholy, and now he's finished. There's no more fire in his life.

I think of a Bible expositor in Central America when my wife was studying Spanish. His series on 1 Corinthians was as good as Ray Stedman or John Stott ever dreamed of doing. Less than ten years later when we were back in that same country for an evangelistic campaign, I met this fellow and his first comment was, 'Luis, how do you keep so excited for God all the time?' I thought then, he's running out of steam. A little while later, he divorced his wife to marry a younger woman. What happened? All that time he had been using the gifts of the Spirit in the power of the flesh, and eventually the flesh runs out of fuel.

Unless you and I are living in the power of God, we're going to run out of petrol. We're going to be cruising along and suddenly lose power. We'll be idled and sidelined, or worse, because we were operating in the flesh.

Many of us were brought up with the concept, 'Now that you're saved, roll up your sleeves. Work for Christ, fight the devil, overcome sin, live for God, grit your teeth, get out there and be a good witness.'

We should be active and fruitful, but in dependence upon a source other than ourself. It doesn't come automatically. But as we consciously depend on God as our ultimate source of power and strength, we're renewed and revitalized. We never have to worry about an energy shortage because God's resources are unlimited.

Look at the example of Robert Murray M'Cheyne, a famous Scottish preacher and man of God. He died when he was only twenty-nine years old. But even as a young man, M'Cheyne was a spiritual giant in Scotland during the last century. They say that when he would get up in the pulpit, people would start crying before he said a single word. Now that's the power of God in someone's life!

On one occasion M'Cheyne told a friend in a letter, 'According to your holiness, so shall be your success.... Mr. Edwards, a holy man is an awesome weapon in the hand of God.' Are we an awesome weapon in the hands of God? We can be, if His power is at work through us.

If you're filled to all the fullness of God, you might not even notice it but you'll have power. Not that you strut around saying, 'I'm filled with the Holy Spirit—watch out! Here comes a man of God. Everybody out of my way.' No, of course not. You just walk, praising God, obeying Him and demonstrating His power with authority. You may not notice anything different, but others will.

What is the key? It's praying, 'Lord, unworthy as I am, I am the temple of God. Please fill this temple completely—for Your glory.' You and I are the temple of God Himself.

By faith will you say, 'Christ lives in me'? Let's see how we can live this each day.

Starting Each Day Renewed

I begin each day with a prayer of thanks to God—as soon as my eyes open and my feet hit the floor. I encourage you to do the same, even on Monday morning.

Beginning your day with a prayer of thanksgiving to God isn't as easy as it sounds. Listen to yourself when you wake up tomorrow morning. For years I groaned about each new day. My prayers, when I prayed, were mostly complaints. 'Lord, here comes another day. I don't feel up to the tasks before me. There are so many temptations. I don't want to lose my temper. Don't let me fail You. Don't let me grieve You. Don't let me dishonour You if an opportunity to witness comes up....' On and on I went, groaning and moaning, wailing and pleading with the Lord.

I remember frequently praying, 'Don't leave me, Lord,' as if He had said just the opposite of Hebrews 13:5–6, 'I am going to leave you and forsake you. Don't count on me. Watch out for what others are going to do to you!' God must have thought my prayers were utter foolishness.

One day Fred Renich, who helped direct our missionary internship programme, challenged us in this area. He claimed that 'most of you probably start out the day groaning. The content, tone and direction of your prayers are negative.' And he was right. I hadn't realized how negative I was.

Renich made it clear he wasn't advocating positive thinking as a cure-all. 'This is different. Pray on the basis of the promises and reality of God.' He urged us to start each day saying things like, 'Thank You, Lord Jesus. Here's a new day. Yes, I'm weak, but You're strong and all Your resources are my resources. I don't always know how to witness to others, but You'll give me the right words. When temptation comes, Lord, I've got Your power. Thank You that You have all power in heaven and on earth. Thank You that You live in me. Thank You that Your resurrection life is real and that today you're going to prove it once again.'

Why start the day with a prayer of unbelief? Why not start with a note of praise? If I understand Romans 4:20 correctly,

Abraham grew strong in his faith as he gave glory to God. God had promised the impossible—his wife, almost ninety years old, would have a son. The temptation to doubt God was incredible. But Abraham became 'fully persuaded that God had power to do what he had promised' (4:21).

Are you convinced that same power of God is in you? Then affirm it at the beginning of each day.

Staying Renewed Throughout the Day

I can hear some people protesting, 'But, Luis, what about the rest of the day? It's one thing to start the day off right. But what about when I face temptation?'

The living Lord Jesus has all the power we'll ever need. The fact that we're cleansed and consecrated and Christ-centered doesn't mean trials and temptations begin bypassing us.

Temptations are a fact of life. Temptations to cheat, to lie, to be shady in business dealings. Temptations to do what might be embarrassing or even shameful. You can get up in the morning, have your devotions, sing a chorus of praise to the Lord, pray, kiss your spouse good-bye, and review a memory verse on the way to work, only to see something you didn't intend to see, or think something you didn't intend to think. Temptation suddenly jumps out at you. What do you do?

Honesty is the best policy. The Lord indwells us and knows every thought. You can say, 'Lord Jesus, thank You that You indwell me. You see what I see. You know how I feel. You know what temptation just hit me. Thank You for Your power at work in me. Thank You for keeping me pure and holy, so that I can give glory to Your name.'

In one of his beautiful hymns, Charles Wesley wrote that Christ 'breaks the power of cancelled sin, He sets the prisoner free'. Temptation loses its grip. 'Sin will have no dominion over you' (Romans 6:14 RSV). Why? Because we're not under the law, trying our best to live for God. Instead, in His grace, 'Christ lives in me.'

There's no place for legalistic Christianity if we're experiencing radical renewal. We don't need a bunch of man-made rules on what to do and what not to do. They aren't necessary because the life of God controls us. That's what makes the Christian life so exciting.

True Christianity is life. It's 'the life of God in the soul of man'. That's the whole reason Jesus came—to give us this life. His desire is that we enjoy it to the full. If He's in your heart, His power is in you, too. The same power that raised Jesus from the dead can give you resurrection life!

When God's resurrection power is at work within us, there's no reason to sweat and try to do the best we can in our own strength. How much better it is when we are available instruments in His hand, letting Christ work through us. Not that we become passive or lazy. If you're renewed, you're probably more active than ever. But in a relaxed way. It's no longer you in charge, you calling all the shots, you trying your hardest. It's 'not I, but Christ living in me'.

It isn't what we do for Christ, but what He does through us. Yes, we work, but not relying on our own power. Yes, we want to walk in the light, but we can't be holy unless He makes us holy. Therefore, we rely on His presence to make us holy and transparent. We couldn't do it on our own, any more than Moses or Paul could on their own. God is there to make it happen.

When we face temptation, therefore, we can say confidently and accurately, 'Sin shall not have dominion over me because I'm not under the law, but under grace.' And grace means that God chose to come and indwell me. It doesn't mean I'm perfect. It doesn't mean I won't stumble at times, especially when it comes to recurring sins. But sin will not dominate me because Christ lives in me and I'm experiencing that reality.

Balanced Every Step of the Way

I often think a man or woman walking in the power of the indwelling Christ is like a tightrope walker. I remember seeing a high wire act when I was a boy in Argentina. Some German performers came and stretched an enormous cable between two buildings over the plaza of the city where I lived. The cable must have been thirty meters off the ground, but the performers didn't set up any safety nets. Starting from opposite ends, they walked across the high wire and played games with the crowd. Everyone thought they were going to fall to their death as they swayed back and forth, used long poles to keep their balance, then traded poles as they tried to get past each other. One of the performers did slip but caught the cable and pulled himself back up. They made it across the high wire in one piece.

Living by the control of the indwelling Lord Jesus is like that. There's a tremendous amount of excitement. People may look at you and say, 'He's not going to make it,' but you keep your balance as you walk with Christ. He's the pole that keeps you in balance every step of the way.

Christ's ultimate objective is to take complete control and mould His character in us. It's not me trying to be holy, trying to be perfect, trying to conform to the image of Christ. It's Christ indwelling and filling me that makes the difference. I'm not passive, but I'm acting in His power. Any power I have is really His in me. Christ has become 'our wisdom, our righteousness and sanctification and redemption' (1 Corinthians 1:30 RSV). No wonder Paul goes on to say, 'Let him who boasts, boast of the Lord' (1:31).

And no wonder Jesus says, 'Let your light shine before men, that they may see your good works and praise your Father in heaven' (Matthew 5:16). The good people see in you and me is Jesus shining through. He is our light, our source of true life. The more we look to Him, the more we 'reflect the Lord's glory' and are 'being transformed into his likeness with ever-increasing glory, which comes from the Lord' (2 Corinthians 3:18).

God is relentlessly at work to transform us; He has no intention of waiting to start the job in heaven. God has already begun His good work in us, and He 'will carry it on to completion until the day of Christ' (Philippians 1:6). His intention is to make us 'conformed to the likeness of his Son' (Romans 8:29).

To think that God is at work within us, filling us with Himself. What a possibility! I can't imagine anything else that will truly transform a person. 'God Himself indwells me.' That alone is a motivation for holy, bold living. That alone compels us to ask, 'Lord, what is on Your heart? How do You want me to feel, act and think? What do You want to do through me here on earth for Your glory?'

This heart-felt prayer leads to the discovery of God's passion—that is, to fill us with His compassion for a lost and hurting world. Out of His radical renewal in our lives comes a desire to take the love of Christ to those who know nothing of it yet. Do you have that passion? Do you want to see God use you to introduce others to His Son? Then hang on! The Christ-centered life naturally leads to heart-felt evangelism.

To Ponder

1. 'Consecration is a critical step towards radical renewal, but it isn't enough. Some people have dedicated and rededicated and super rededicated their lives to God. But they still feel anything but renewed.' Have you ever longed for a touch of God on your life? Have you ever wanted to feel His presence at work within you? What prompted that desire?

2. 'The only person who could ever live the Christian life was Christ Himself.' What happens if we try to live for God in our own strength? Has that ever happened to you?

3. 'The cross was a necessary prerequisite for God's ultimate objective, which is to unite us with Himself forever.' Why do you think God wants to fill us? What will we be like when He's through?

4. 'We experience God's renewal within us when you and I

not only understand but also accept this truth—Christ literally lives in us!' Why isn't consecration enough? What difference does the Christ-centered life make?

5. 'Most Christians know nothing of the fullness of God. They have never experienced the joy and power and victory of the Christ-centered life.' Why do you think that's true? What prevents most Christians from enjoying this tremendous possibility?

6. 'The Bible teaches that if you want a fruitful life, if you want victory to overcome temptation, if you want power and authority, then it can't be you. It must be Christ!' Have you discovered the revolutionary impact of the Christ-centered life yet? If so, what positive changes has it made in you, your ministry and your relationships with others?

7. 'As we consciously depend on God as our ultimate source of power and strength, we're renewed and revitalized. We never have to worry about an energy shortage because God's resources are unlimited.' If this is true in our lives, how will we start each day? How will we stay renewed throughout the day? What's the secret for keeping balanced every step of the way?

To Pursue

1. Turn in your Bible to Ephesians 3:14–19 and read it, out loud if possible. Then take your pen and underline the last phrase of the prayer—'that you may be filled to all the fullness of God'. Ask God to make this true in your life and experience.

2. Take ten minutes to begin underlining other New Testament verses, especially in the Gospel of John and the epistles, that speak of God filling us with Himself. Start with John 15:5 and 17:21–23, then underline 1 Corinthians 6:17, Galatians 2:20, Ephesians 5:18, Philippians 4:12, Colossians 1:27 and 2:9–10. Underline other verses as you find them in days ahead.

3. Turn in your Bible to Exodus 3 and review the story

about Moses and the burning bush. Picture what the bush must have looked like when God was in it. Then picture the fire disappearing, leaving the dried-up old bush alone again in the desert. Finally, picture the bush later turning to ash in a shepherd's fire. Which picture best describes you?

4. With every sin confessed, and every area of your life consecrated to God, ask Him to fill every fibre of your being. Be sure to thank Him for that filling now and again later today several more times.

5. During the next six weeks establish a new habit. Begin each day with a prayer of thanks to God. Reaffirm the many promises of God and claim them anew each morning. Especially thank the Lord for His presence and reality in your life.

CHAPTER 8

THE CONCERNED LIFE

*When we're filled with God, our hearts are
burdened by the same things that burden His heart.
What's on God's heart? First and foremost, He's
concerned about reconciling people to Himself....*

God-filled people come in a lot of shapes and disguises.
During preparation for one of our evangelistic campaigns in
Latin America some years ago, a very poor, shoeless,
unshaven, shabbily dressed man attended one of our week-
long Biblical Counselling courses.

Generally, the better educated, socially established, and
spiritually mature lay leaders of the local churches in a city
attend this in-depth training course. So it was unusual to see
such a poor man participating, especially because he was
illiterate.

Although the man attended every class, we didn't expect
him to do much counselling. Like many illiterate people,
however, he had a fantastic memory. Little did we realize how
much he really knew.

Several weeks later, every available counsellor at our family
counselling centre was busy except the illiterate man. Just
then a doctor walked in, requesting counsel. In Latin America, most doctors are very sophisticated and fashionable, and
this doctor was no exception.

Before anyone could stop him, the shabbily dressed man
took the doctor into a room for counselling. When our counselling director found out what had happened, he was a bit

concerned to say the least. When the doctor came out of the counselling room, the director asked if he could help him in any way.

'No, thank you,' the doctor replied. 'This fellow has helped me very much.'

The next day the doctor returned for counselling with two other doctors. Our counselling director wanted to talk with them, but the doctor refused, asking for counsel with the shoeless, illiterate man. By the end of the week, that illiterate man had led four doctors and their wives to Christ! What a glorious servant of Jesus Christ! He couldn't read or write, but he lived a victorious Christian life.

So often we look on the outside when measuring someone else's spirituality. What really counts is the power of the living Christ within. That's the secret to radical renewal, as we saw in the last chapter. Overflowing from such renewal comes a deep, growing, heartfelt passion for the things of God.

When we're filled with God, our hearts are burdened by the same things that burden His heart. What's on God's heart? First and foremost, He's concerned about reconciling people to Himself. The Lord isn't willing that any perish, but wants everyone to come to repentance (2 Peter 3:9). How can we get that same overriding passion for lost souls?

Genuine concern for the lost doesn't come naturally. By nature we're selfish. As long as we have our own little goodies, we're happy. But when you're filled with God, it isn't long before you say, 'God, give me a passion to see people come to know You. You've done so much for me. I want everyone to experience Your salvation and see You at work in his life.'

When someone enjoys the filling of God, no one has to force him to do evangelism. It's a supernatural byproduct of radical renewal. If someone doesn't have a passion for the lost, on the other hand, don't try to make him witness for Christ. If we don't share the Gospel from the heart, we almost invariably make a mess of it. People end up needlessly turned off to Jesus Christ instead of trusting Him as Saviour.

A passion for the lost isn't something we're taught. I'm all for motivating and training Christians for evangelism. In fact, part of my evangelistic association's vision is 'to stimulate, revive and mobilize the Church to continuous, effective evangelism, follow-up and church growth'. Thousands of people take our friendship evangelism training course before our evangelistic campaigns. And a good number then have the opportunity to lead someone to Jesus Christ. But training itself can't stir a concern for the destiny of lost souls.

When the Holy Spirit is flowing through our lives, we automatically begin to share the Gospel with others. Jesus told His disciples, 'You will receive power when the Holy Spirit comes on you; and you will be my witnesses....' (Acts 1:8). And that's exactly what happened. Formerly timid Galileans became holy, bold witnesses for His name. The same can be true in our lives today.

My father-in-law is such a quiet guy I can't imagine him saying more than a couple of lines trying to witness to his old college buddies, for whom he has such a burden. But anytime I'm speaking in town, he brings one or more of them. He could never be a public speaker, and he doesn't want to be. That's not what a passion for the lost is all about.

Some people complain, 'I don't have the gift of evangelism. I could never preach the Gospel like you do, Luis.' You don't have to. But you can have the same deep heart of compassion for the lost. The secret isn't in striving to get some gift God never intended to give you. Instead, the secret is living and witnessing by the power of the indwelling Lord. That's true whether you're a Sunday school teacher who takes a special concern for that one lost kid in your class, or a talented musician who uses her musical gift to the glory of God.

The Bible says, 'He who is faithful in a very little thing is faithful also in much' (Luke 16:10 NASB). Be faithful where you are, and the Lord will begin to open doors for you. When you witness as an overflow from a heart filled by God's Spirit, people sense your love and concern.

Day of the Laid Back Evangelical

Tragically, a gripping passion for the lost is a rare commodity in the Church today. This is the day of the laid back evangelical. I heard a speaker at my church say, 'When I was younger I worked with Campus Crusade. I used to buttonhole everybody. I used to witness to anything that moved, and even some things that didn't move.'

The speaker was trying to be funny, and implying that he'd 'matured' beyond that point. However, in the last thirty years I've never been buttonholed by a Christian. I wish somebody would try to witness to me. Billy Graham said that in the days of the Jesus People movement, he walked down the Sunset Strip in Hollywood and in one three-block stretch was buttonholed three times. It made him weep. It would make me weep.

I wish people were actively witnessing for Christ. Why do Christians sometimes make fun of such things? Because people love to hear sarcastic remarks. They want to be laid back. But how can we have that attitude when people go to hell?

The closest anyone has come to buttonholing me was in London. I was walking down a street with one of our British board members when we came to a street fair. Thousands of people were crowded together. No sooner had I said, 'Someone should be passing out invitations to our campaign,' than a young man gave me an invitation. I said, 'Hello, brother, thanks for doing this. I'm Luis Palau.' Other than that, no one has witnessed to me since my college days.

Why do the majority of Christians lack any concern for the unsaved? Because they've never experienced God's radical renewal in their life. 'Come, follow me,' Jesus said, 'and I will make you fishers of men' (Matthew 4:19). It's only as we wholeheartedly follow Christ Jesus that we gain His passion for the lost.

Cultivating a Heart of Compassion

As followers of Christ, what can we do to cultivate His heart of compassion for those who are 'harassed and helpless, like sheep without a shepherd' (Matthew 9:36)?

First, we can pray. 'The harvest is plentiful but the workers are few. Ask the Lord of the harvest, therefore, to send out workers into his harvest field' (Matthew 9:37–38). We can pray for workers, both for those already actively involved in evangelism and cross-cultural missions, and for those yet to be sent out.

We can also pray for those who have yet to trust Jesus Christ. Make a list of the unsaved family members, friends, neighbours, and others you know from school or work who need Christ. Get on your knees and pray regularly for each person by name. Be persistent in your prayers. Think long-term. To God, no amount of time is too long to pray for someone.

My wife and I know an elderly woman who prayed for sixty-eight years for her brother's salvation. When he was eighty years old, shortly before he died, he confessed the Lord Jesus as Saviour. Someone may think, 'That was by the skin of his teeth!' but the benefit was not only his. Imagine the tremendous blessing in that woman's life resulting from sixty-eight years of faithful praying.

Of course, sometimes God answers our prayers quite quickly. A friend took up my challenge to pray by name for the salvation of five businessmen he knows. Then we got together for lunch a few weeks later. The Lord had already given him the opportunity to witness to one of those five business friends, who surrendered his life to Jesus Christ. You can imagine how excited my friend was. And you'd better believe he wants to keep praying for the other four men.

A teenage girl I met in Scotland accepted a similar challenge, praying by name for ten of her friends at school. Within a year all ten had trusted Jesus Christ as Saviour. This girl was elated. Many others have told me similar stories.

Second, study what the Bible says about eternity. Read all

the passages in the New Testament that talk about the eternal condemnation of the lost. What you'll discover is Scripture teaches that those who reject Jesus Christ to their dying day go to hell—'the lake of fire'.

Note what Jesus Himself says in the Gospels: 'Do not be afraid of those who kill the body but cannot kill the soul. Rather, be afraid of the one [God] who can destroy both soul and body in hell' (Matthew 10:28).

On many occasions Jesus warned about being 'in danger of the fire of hell' or being 'thrown into hell'. Concerning His Church, Jesus said, 'the gates of Hades will not overcome it' (Matthew 16:18).

In some of His harshest words, Jesus calls the hypocritical religious leaders in Jerusalem and their disciples 'son[s] of hell' (Matthew 23:15) and asked them, 'How will you escape being condemned to hell?' (23:33).

Third, believe implicitly what the Bible says about the eternal condition of the lost. Let His words about the hopelessness and agony of the lost sink in. The Lord speaks of hell as a place of weeping, wailing, and gnashing of teeth.

Some try to explain away what the Bible teaches about hell. 'If people die rejecting Christ, are they really going to be lost forever?' Yes. But it takes a while for us to believe that. Most of us would like to believe that somehow, at the end of history, after people have been in hell for a thousand years, the Lord will say, 'Let's have a general amnesty. Let's bring the poor souls up to paradise.'

That's not what the Bible teaches, but that's what so many, even in evangelical circles, would like to believe. And that's why many Christians don't have a passion for souls. We refuse to believe that if someone rejects Christ up to his dying day, he's really lost forever and there's no hope.

If we believed the Bible implicitly, our thinking would change dramatically. Instead of halfheartedly wishing an unsaved friend or relative would be saved, we would realize, 'If he has an accident and dies tomorrow, he's going to hell forever.' When that hits home, it's cause for concern and drives us to want to win that person to Christ.

If we believe what the Bible says about the lost, we're going to want to spend time alone with God. We're going to pray, 'God, give me a passion for those who don't know You yet. Teach me the value of a soul.' I did that thirty-five years ago and haven't felt laid back since then. How can I stay home, comfortable and content, while I know where people go when they die without Christ? How can we do nothing?

Developing a Life-style of Soul-winning

The Bible says, 'The fruit of the righteous is a tree of life, and he who wins souls is wise' (Proverbs 11:30). I know this verse is batted around as if it had nothing to do with a passion for the lost. Let's carefully look at what it says.

First, if we are righteous, if we are walking with God in the light of His presence, then we're a tree of life. And what greater fruit could anyone bear than bringing the message of eternal life to those he or she loves? Some of your friends and relatives who don't know the Lord may seem hardened against the Gospel. From your perspective, it may appear there is no apparent hope for their conversion. But don't become unconcerned or apathetic. Continue to live righteously because 'the fruit of the righteous is a tree of life'. This tree brings forth fruit in its season.

Second, God says, 'And he (or she) who wins souls is wise.' I've heard people say that phrase is outdated, but it's still in the Bible and I happen to like it. Scripture says God created man, breathed into him and he became 'a living soul' (Genesis 2:7). You and I are living souls. Someday our bodies will fall apart. No amount of medicine or vitamins or exercise can prevent that from happening. But our soul lives forever. It never dies. That's why the Bible says he or she who wins souls is wise.

There's no greater joy than saying, 'That person, and that person, and that person—the Lord used me to win them to

Jesus Christ.' We've already talked about making a list of people you want to see saved. If you've been radically renewed, watch God begin to use you to win some of them to Christ. It's a fantastic joy.

Winning people to Christ is the greatest joy. Your graduation is exciting, your wedding is exciting, the birth of your first child is exciting. But the most thrilling thing you and I can ever do is win someone to Christ.

Even the very best the world has to offer is nothing compared to finding Jesus Christ and leading others to Him. I think of Fiona Hendley-Jones, an actress who shot to fame as one of the three women robbers in TV's hit series *Widows*, and later starred in *The Beggar's Opera* and *Guys and Dolls*, both with former pop idol turned actor Paul Jones.

Cliff Richard invited both Fiona and Paul to one of our evangelistic campaign meetings in London several years ago. They trusted Jesus Christ and shortly thereafter were married. Their acting careers continued to meet with huge success. But they joined a strong evangelical church and since have repeatedly commented in public appearances and media interviews about their new life in Christ.

'A lot of people turn to the Church when they have torments in their life, but I was deliriously happy,' Fiona explained while witnessing to one reporter. She told him how her life had 'completely changed [when] I became a born-again Christian'. Her testimony has helped lead many people to Christ.

God wants to use each of us, famous or not, to tell others about the Good News. Your testimony may not be dramatic. Mine isn't either. That doesn't matter. As Jesus told His disciples, let's simply rejoice that our name is written in the book of life as we tell others how they, too, can know they have eternal life.

The Dutch evangelist Corrie ten Boom had a God-given desire to win others to Christ. I had the privilege of meeting her before she died several years ago. One of her poems is a favourite of mine. It says, 'When I enter that beautiful city /

And the saints all around me appear, / I hope that someone will tell me: / "It was you who invited me here." '

Can you imagine? To get to heaven and meet someone who comes up and gives you a big hug and says, 'Hey, I'm here because you invited me.' Nothing else could compare with that thrill!

Getting Started

You may be saying, 'Luis, how do I begin?' Why not begin with your interests and associations. If you're interested in football, befriend the people in your area who play football or attend the matches. If you're in a school car pool, pray for the parents and kids in your car pool.

If you enjoy fishing, invite a neighbour to go with you and pray for an opportunity to talk about the Gospel. If you belong to a business or community group, pray to be used to win someone in that group for Christ. If you host an exchange student from another country, you may have an excellent opportunity to witness for Christ right in your own home.

If you work at an office or factory, you may know a dozen people or more who need Christ. The same is true if you're going to school. Pray for those you know by name. Don't rush to witness to the next person you meet. Begin to pray and the Holy Spirit will prompt you and give you an opportunity to share the love of Christ with specific individuals.

Maybe a family is going through the heartache of divorce. When they mention it to you, invite them to pray with you. They may not be ready to trust Christ on the spot. But by praying with them, they'll know you love them. Then watch for an opportunity to share the love of Christ with them.

If you're prayerfully alert, you may discover a large number of people around you who need Christ. You may find incredible opportunities to witness. I think of Martha who wrote to our evangelistic team, asking us to pray for her new neighbours, Dan and Annette. Before moving next door to Martha, this couple had never heard the Gospel or read the

Bible. Martha immediately befriended them, enlisted friends to pray for them, and then invited Annette over each week for an evangelistic Bible study.

Recently we received another letter from Martha. Her neighbour Annette has prayed to receive Jesus Christ, she told us, 'and now He is already working in her husband's heart. Dan has attended worship services for the past three weeks and is desiring to know Christ as his personal Saviour as well.' Praise God! You can know the same joy, too.

How Can We Remain Complacent?

If God is in our hearts, if He's blessed our life, if heaven is our home, how can we remain complacent about the destiny of our lost neighbours, relatives and friends? Can we care nothing about their present state? To think that the lost are happy 'just as they are' is naive. They're lonely, hurting, desperate for love, and dying for a reason to live.

A young man in Toronto, Canada, named Steve trusted Christ a couple of years ago. When we were back in that city recently, one of my team members interviewed Steve about his conversion. 'I remember that Friday night very well— January 15,' he said. 'I was suicidal and bitter at life, particularly at my family. I couldn't care about anything. When Luis said to come forward, I jumped at the chance. Ever since then I've been witnessing at my school—it's been a joy in my life. And a lot of people have become Christians. What happens is, you tell someone about Jesus and he becomes a Christian and tells someone else. Miracles happen!' That same night, three more of Steve's friends trusted the Lord at a Youth for Christ rally where I spoke. It was exciting to hear his story and see how God has blessed him with so much fruit.

Yet today, in an effort to be sophisticated and contemporary, many Christians have stopped trying to persuade others to follow Christ. There's an underlying feeling in our society that nice people don't go around persuading other people to do things. We don't want to offend people, appear strange, or lose our status. So we do nothing.

I, too, have been guilty of this. When we lived in Mexico City, my next-door neighbour was a young television personality. We would chat from time to time, and he even mentioned that he listened to our radio programme occasionally. But I didn't share the Gospel with him. I thought, he seems completely immune to the problems of life.

Eventually, though, my neighbour's situation changed. The joy seemed to have left his face. He and his wife started driving separate cars to work. I could tell their marriage was souring, and I felt the need to talk with him. But I didn't want to meddle in his life. I went about my business and headed off for an evangelistic campaign in Peru. After all, that was the polite thing to do.

When I returned home, I learned my neighbour had killed himself. I was heartbroken. I knew I should have gone to him and persuaded him to repent and follow Christ. But because of false courtesy—because I followed a social norm—I didn't do it.

It's very convenient to make excuses for not persuading others to follow Christ. We may say we don't want to be overbearing or offensive. We may think we can't possibly witness to someone because he or she will become angry. But often the opposite is true.

I think of my daughter-in-law's experience as a college student. Michelle met a young woman who lived in the same apartment complex, and felt compelled to invite her to an evangelistic rally where I was speaking. Her neighbour said 'yes' just like that. Michelle didn't have to twist her arm or beg her or sell her on the idea. She just came, sat down, and listened to the Gospel.

When I closed my message and gave the invitation, using Revelation 3:20, Michelle's new friend stood and almost ran forward to confess the Lord. Later she said, 'For years I've felt somebody knocking at the door of my heart, but I never knew who it was.' Incredibly, she had never heard the Gospel until that night. But as soon as she did hear it, she embraced it wholeheartedly.

Jesus longs to draw men and women to Himself. What holds us back from speaking to others in His name?

People Often Welcome the Gospel Message

Over the years I have learned that some of the people I thought would be most closed to the Gospel often are the most receptive. They may outwardly fear it, but in their hearts they welcome the message of the Gospel.

I saw this while in the Soviet Union a few months before the dramatic collapse of communism in Eastern Europe. Christians in the Soviet Union, like other communist countries, had been persecuted for decades. Then restrictions on evangelism were lifted. The situation I found there was incredible. I've travelled all over the world, but I've rarely seen a place as hungry and desperate to hear the Gospel. Yet it took a while for many Soviet Christians to realize 'the fields are white already to harvest'.

Just before my evangelistic team's Soviet campaign was over, a Baptist pastor brought an acquaintance to one of our meetings in Moscow. The friend, a leading scientist and head of an academic department at the university, listened as I preached the Gospel. To the pastor's surprise, this scientist prayed out loud to receive Jesus Christ as his Saviour. Then, with tears, he came forward to confess Christ publicly.

The Russian pastor was astonished at his friend's response to the Gospel. He was equally surprised by the phone call he received at 7:15 the next morning. 'I would like to express my gratitude to you,' the scientist said. 'You invited me to meet the Lord Jesus Christ. I didn't sleep the whole night. I just prayed. I asked God whether He would accept me, whether He would pardon me.'

'Well, do you think God pardoned you?' the pastor asked.

His friend replied, 'Yes, I'm absolutely sure that God accepts me as His prodigal son.'

Later the pastor told me, 'I never thought a scientist would accept the Lord Jesus as Saviour. But now I've seen it with my own eyes. What a great experience!'

Why Do We Hold Back?

Having a part in leading a friend or acquaintance to faith in Jesus Christ is exciting. Actually praying with someone who wants to make that decision is even more thrilling. Yet I've seen Christians panic when they're talking with someone who's at the point of decision, ready to trust Christ.

A Christian woman was witnessing to a Hungarian businesswoman sitting in front of me on a flight from Budapest to London. At the same time our team's European director and I were discussing the evangelistic rally we had in Budapest the day before together with Cliff Richard.

While we were talking the Christian woman stood up, turned around and said, 'Excuse me. Are you talking about the rally yesterday with Cliff Richard and Luis Palau?' I said yes. 'Do you know where brother Palau is?' I said that was me. 'I've been talking to this Hungarian lady, and I think she's ready to be converted. But I don't know how to do it.'

I told her, 'I've been listening to what you've been saying and you're doing a terrific job.' But she feared doing something wrong when it came time to pray with someone who was ready to receive Christ. So I agreed to talk with the Hungarian businesswoman for a minute.

'Did you understand what this lady said to you?' I asked.

'Yes,' said the Hungarian woman.

'Are you ready to open the door of your life to Christ?'

'Yes.'

At that, I asked the Christian woman to lead her in a prayer of decision. I wanted to do it myself; it would have been great. Instead, I sat back and watched as the Christian woman in front of me at first hesitated, then put her arm around this Hungarian woman, and for the first time led someone to Christ.

I challenge you to pray: 'Dear God, I want that experience. I want to know what it is to win someone to Jesus Christ.'

Oh, to have a passion for the lost! Why should we be ashamed of the Gospel? 'It is the power of God for the salvation of everyone who believes' (Romans 1:16). It changes lives here and now, and for eternity. Whatever our place in the Body of Christ, let's work together to actively and prayerfully invite others into God's kingdom.

The Lord never intended Christian life and witness to be a solo act, of course. How can you and I prayerfully promote radical renewal and a passion for the lost within our churches, throughout our cities, and eventually across this land? That's the challenge ahead.

To Ponder

1. 'When we're filled with God, our hearts are burdened by the same things that burden His heart.' What's on God's heart? Do you feel that same compassion?

2. 'When the Holy Spirit is flowing through our lives, we automatically begin to share the Gospel with others.' Jesus foretold this in Acts 1:8. Can you think of any examples of this mentioned later in the book of Acts? What is the lesson for today?

3. This is the day of the laid back evangelical. Why do you think Christians sometimes make sarcastic remarks about evangelism? Why do most lack a genuine concern for the lost? What makes people so complacent?

4. 'If someone rejects Christ up to his dying day, he's lost forever and there's no hope.' Do you believe that? Why or why not?

5. 'How can I stay home, comfortable and content, while I know where people go when they die without Christ? How can I do nothing?' What has been your response in the past? What is your desire now?

6. 'Your graduation is exciting, your wedding is exciting, the birth of your first child is exciting. But the most thrilling

thing you and I can ever do is win someone to Christ.' Have you ever had that experience? Have you tried to win someone to Christ who turned around and rejected the offer of salvation? Do you think the average person is close-minded or receptive to the Gospel message?

7. A renewed life marked by the blessing of God is a powerful witness to a watching world. In what areas of life does God want to bless us? Does that mean we're exempt from trials and temptations? What's the difference between a renewed Christian and someone else? How is that demonstrated as we talk to those who don't know Christ?

To Pursue

1. In your notebook, make a list of people you know who are already actively involved in evangelism and cross-cultural missions. Specify which group of people they are trying to reach, and begin praying regularly for them to see much fruit. Also ask God 'to send out more workers into his harvest field' (Matthew 9:38).

2. Make a list of people you know who have yet to trust Jesus Christ. Begin praying earnestly for your unsaved family members, friends, neighbours, and others you know from school or work who need Christ. Ask others to join you in praying for the salvation of these people.

3. Study what the Bible says about the eternal condemnation of the lost, and write down your observations in your notebook. Begin with one of the following groups of verses:

* In the Old Testament—Deuteronomy 32:21–22; Job 10:20–22; Daniel 12:2.

* In the Gospel of Matthew—5:22, 5:29–30, 7:22–23, 8:12, 10:28, 11:23, 13:41–42, 13:49–50, 16:18, 18:9, 23:15, 23:33, 25:31–33, 25:41–46.

* In the other Gospels—Mark 8:36, 9:43–47; Luke 9:25, 10:15, 12:5, 16:23; John 3:17–18, 3:36, 5:28–29.

* In the epistles—Romans 2:5; Philippians 3:19; 2 The-

ssalonians 1:7–9; Hebrews 6:2, 10:39; James 3:6; 2 Peter 2:4, 2:7, 3:9; Jude 6, 7, 13.

  * In Revelation—1:18, 2:11, 9:2, 9:11, 19:20, 20:6, 20:10, 20:13–15, 21:8.

  4. In prayer, tell the Lord what you've learned about hell. Ask Him to give you a passion for those who don't know Christ yet. Ask Him to teach you the value of a soul. Pray that you'll have the opportunity to winsomely present the Gospel to someone during the next month.

  5. Actively and prayerfully pursue opportunities to talk to others about Christ. In your notebook, list at least three strategies you could pursue in your neighbourhood, at school or work, and elsewhere in your community. Begin implementing one of the strategies this week. Ask the Lord to bless you and use you to lead someone to Himself.

CHAPTER 9

THE CHALLENGE AHEAD

*What could God do in our church, city, and
even country for His glory?
We'll never know if we ignore the principles of
radical renewal or keep them to ourselves....*

God desires to radically renew you and me. Overflowing
from such renewal comes an increasingly intense passion for
the things of God.

First and foremost, the Lord gives us a passion for lost
souls. We can't lay back and remain complacent; we must
share His blessings with others.

We actively and prayerfully seek opportunities to be used
by the Lord to win others to Himself.

But secondly, the Lord gives us a passion for His Church.
You see, God's plan is much bigger than His plan for you and
me alone. In some ways, it's even bigger than His burden for
the world. Yes, He earnestly desires to draw men and women
and young people to Himself. But why? To build up and bless
the Church.

What's so special about the Church? From God's perspective, a lot. We may look around at the tiny representative
portion of the Church near us and condemn the warts,
wrinkles, and blemishes.

But God sees the whole Church, throughout the world,
down through the ages and into eternity. He views us not
only as His special creation and masterpiece, but also as His
family. God's ultimate goal is to perfect the Church and

gather us all together (along with all the Old Testament saints) to spend eternity with Him in heaven.

The highlight in heaven won't be the streets of gold, but the fact that God wants to dwell with us forever (Revelation 21:3). He's not satisfied just to indwell us and fill us here on earth. He wants us to live 'face to face' with Him (1 Corinthians 13:12). 'We shall be like him' in that day, 'for we shall see him as he is' (1 John 3:2).

Granted, we in the Church aren't all we should be, or all we one day will be when we're with the Lord in glory. That doesn't change the fact that He is doing a good work within us. His goal is to renew both individuals and local churches here on earth.

God Wants to Renew His Church

What constitutes a renewed local church? Getting very specific, what would Crest View Church, which we examined at the beginning of the book, look like when it is renewed? Here's how I define a renewed church: a congregation where a majority of the members understand the principles of radical renewal and live them out.

The work of God in such churches is often astounding. Some hard-hearted souls will resist renewal. But I believe most Christians would give anything to be part of a church experiencing radical renewal. There is nothing more exciting than to be part of a thriving, growing congregation that is obviously moved by God.

If we really want to see renewal in our churches, if we want to see God radically transform His Church across this land, we must say 'yes!' to His work in our own lives. Otherwise, how can we promote what we ourselves haven't experienced? How can we present what we don't know and have?

Although I've talked a lot about 'you and me', this book is meant for the whole Body of Christ. Writing these chapters has been good for me. I've had to pray, 'Lord, am I living up to this message? I've enjoyed a Christ-centered life. I've seen great touches of renewal bless Your Church in various places. Am I living at that same level today? And, in fact, have I been growing in my walk with You?'

I trust this book has also been used of God to make an impact in your own life. But don't be content to keep the principles of radical renewal to yourself. An independent, private, secretive Christianity works, but its progress is slow. Endeavour to live out these biblical principles in your spheres of life and begin presenting them to those in your extended family, circle of friends, and church fellowship. You may be surprised what God starts to do.

An Overall Strategy for Church Growth

Have you ever dreamed about what God wants to do— starting with you—in your church, in your city? I believe God wants to use you. If you're experiencing renewal in your own life, prayerfully consider how this material could be presented to others in your home Bible study, Sunday school class, or church as a whole.

Ideally, the principles of radical renewal should be presented as part of an overall strategy for church growth. Here's a strategy I like to use.

First, introduce radical renewal. This can be done during a week of meetings or through a series of Sunday messages. Begin by presenting the possibilities of the Christian life (chapter 3). Then discuss why those possibilities aren't achieved (chapter 4). Give the principles of cleansing (chapter 5) and consecration (chapter 6). But don't stop there! Go on to discuss the key to radical renewal—Christ in you, living through you (chapter 7)—and finally, how this will produce a passion for the lost (chapter 8).

Second, after you see evidences of renewal, begin presenting the Gospel. Working with renewed believers, plan specialized outreaches for children, youth, singles, couples, families, and senior citizens. Also think of creative ways to reach out to professional groups such as athletes and artists.

By targeting specific affinity groups, people in your church will feel more comfortable inviting their non-Christian friends to these outreaches. Use neutral locations to make the events even less threatening.

Third, when people begin trusting Jesus Christ as Saviour, build them up in their newfound faith. Form small nurture groups where newer Christians can meet together with several older Christians on a weekly basis. Talk about how to read and study the Bible, how to talk to God, how to become part of your local church, how to share your faith with others. Cover all the basics as if they'd never even heard of Scripture, prayer, fellowship or witnessing before.

Following Christ is a cross-cultural experience for most people. The day someone comes to Christ, he or she is spiritually transformed. But socially and intellectually, many new Christians soon discover they're living in foreign territory. They can go through culture shock, if we're not careful.

In befriending new Christians, however, we shouldn't wait too long before introducing the principles of confession, cleansing, consecration and the Christ-centered life to them. Why should they have to struggle for years before learning how to enjoy the Christian life? Why should they repeat the mistakes of countless millions of unrenewed Christians?

The biblical principles presented in this book are deep, yet simple. They're deep enough to challenge us for a lifetime, yet they're simple enough for most people to understand and apply immediately. And they work no matter where we apply them.

Renewal Firsthand in a Local Church Setting

I remember the first time I was invited to test this strategy for ongoing renewal and evangelism in a local church setting. God had already radically changed my own life and given me a tremendous passion for the lost. I was convinced God could renew the Church through big citywide evangelistic campaigns. But I was in my early thirties and wondering if God would use me to reach the masses. I knew if it was going to work on that scale, it would have to work in small churches, too. La Floresta Presbyterian Church in Cali, Colombia, was where I conducted my first test.

I was invited by a missionary, who doubled as the pastor of La Floresta, to minister to his congregation of about sixty members. Joining me was a missionary colleague who served as song leader, and an inspiring young national named Libny. Libny had assisted with our street meetings in Cali, and I found him to be an enthusiastic, dedicated, prayerful young man.

Libny and I prayed for hours about the campaign, and we were finally convinced that God was about to bring renewal to the church. We knew that the best way to inspire the church for evangelism is to make sure the Christians are cleansed and walking in the power of the Spirit.

A Christian who is out of fellowship with God might invite people to the meetings and cooperate with our efforts out of a sense of duty, or the realization that he will betray his spiritual bankruptcy if he doesn't. But, when he's out there talking to people, rather than dying with Christ he's more likely to be dying of embarrassment.

My plan was the one I just outlined, and still use today. Naturally, the first night I wanted the Christians at La Floresta to be tantalized by the possibilities of the Christian life. On the second night, I planned to address why so many Christians miss out on all those tremendous possibilities. I believe in the Keswick approach: if you can provoke a crisis in someone's spiritual life, you can drive him or her back to God. I wanted the Christians to go home from the meeting so ashamed of themselves and repentant over carnality in their lives that they would be ready to be renewed as we continued the series.

It didn't quite work out the way I planned. In fact, we almost didn't make it past the second night.

Breakthrough at La Floresta

I started the message that night to a packed crowd of 200 by reading from Matthew 5:23–24 about settling disputes with your brothers before you bring your offering to the altar. I then talked about the little sins and was ready to move into the the big ones that destroy homes and families. Suddenly a man stood and shouted, 'Wait a minute! This is enough!'

Libny, sitting on the platform behind me, immediately began to pray. He felt, as I did, that we were about to have either a scandal or a revival. 'I'm an elder of this church,' the man said. 'But my family is a mess, and I'm an embarrassment to this church.

'I've got to confess my sins right now. My wife and I don't get along, and my children disobey me. Look at me! I'm seated here, my wife's over there, and my children are back there somewhere. Wife, please come here! Children, please come here!'

As that family, weeping and broken, came together, people all over the tiny, steaming, crowded sanctuary began popping to their feet to confess their sins. I was speechless and scared. I had asked for renewal, but not this way—this wasn't the tradition I had grown up in. I ordered the windows closed and for only church members and other Christians to remain. The confession continued.

In the middle of it all, a man rose and said loudly, 'My turn! You know that young man on the platform?' he announced, pointing at Libny. 'I caused his father's death. He died of a heart attack, but I am responsible, because when we were both elders we had a violent personal disagreement. There's nothing I can do about it now, but....' He broke down and wept. Finally, he blurted, 'I want to ask young Libny, right here in public, if he will forgive me on behalf of his father.'

'Libny,' I asked, 'are you going to forgive this man?' Libny went down to the man and embraced him. For nearly two hours, the congregation publicly confessed its sins and got right with God. What we had hoped and prayed for had happened.

Later that week, we asked for a public confession of the congregation's desire to present their bodies as living sacrifices to God. Almost everyone in the church came forward. Then at the end of that week, with the Christians renewed and anxious to get on with the work of evangelism, we moved our meetings outside to a patio area and presented the Gospel with power to the community at large.

People came from all over that part of Cali for the evangelistic meetings at La Floresta. More than 125 people trusted Jesus Christ, and about 80 joined that particular congregation.

Libny and I could hardly sleep those two weeks. We walked around the town at night, praying and dreaming big dreams for the future. La Floresta Presbyterian Church remained in a state of continual renewal for many months, marked by spontaneous evangelism and joy. If God could do such a tremendous work in one little church, what else could He do? Little did I know that fifteen months after the La Floresta campaign, my mission would give me permission to form my own evangelistic team.

Breakthroughs Around the World

Since then, I've become even more convinced that God wants to renew His Church in this country and around the world. I've seen it happen across the Americas, in parts of Europe and Asia, too.

About a year ago I had the privilege of meeting a Lutheran minister whose church has been seeing someone come to the Lord almost every week. But this pastor would be the first to admit that during his first eleven years of full-time ministry, he had led only one person to Jesus Christ—and he doubts even that one.

But God renewed this pastor while we were preparing for an evangelistic campaign in his city. He heard me present the principles outlined in this book, and then completed our evangelistic association's friendship evangelism, counsellor and follow-up leader training courses.

This pastor's passion for the lost grew still deeper during the campaign itself. He served as both a counsellor and a pastoral advisor at the stadium meetings, helping many people clarify their public commitment to the Lord.

'I had been preaching evangelism,' he realized during the campaign, 'but not practising it.' About a week later, that changed. During a pre-marital counselling session, this Lutheran minister asked a young couple if they had eternal life. They said no. Instead of just talking about their need to trust Jesus Christ, he invited them to make that decision right there in his office.

Within six months, this pastor had led more than twenty other people to Christ. What began as renewal in one pastor's life has produced a fabulous breakthrough in his church. And God has given him opportunities to help other churches experience spiritual and numerical growth, too.

'I don't think my feet have hit the ground yet,' he remarked. 'This is the beginning of a real revival for our congregation.' That's the fruit of a renewed life overflowing with a passion for the things of God.

Imagine what God could do in your church, and my church, for His glory in coming months. We'll never know if we ignore the principles of radical renewal or keep them to ourselves.

If God renews you, you'll grow to love your church and pray for her. And you'll pray for the Church around the world. You won't have a sectarian bone in your body. Or if you do, you'll crucify it. Because if we're renewed, we're diligent to do whatever God commands. And one of the primary commands repeated eight times for us in the New Testament is to 'love one another'. That applies to all Christians, across the board, whether or not we agree on every point of doctrine and practice.

When I was younger, I used to preach certain minor points of doctrine with conviction. Now I'm embarrassed because after much further prayer and study I've changed my mind about a few of those details. What I'd learned earlier sounded good, but wasn't based squarely on a balanced view of God and His Word. So I've grown, which is good. Let's leave room for others to grow, too.

Let's strive for the unity of the Body of Christ. Let's love our brothers and sisters in Christ, pray for them, and respect them as His Word commands. We won't see eye to eye on everything. But we can have unity because we were bought by the blood of the Saviour, we're filled with His Spirit, and we're preaching His Word. That's our common ground, our basis for unity with all who are called by His name.

My prayer is that God will use this book to bless the whole Church. May He renew us all and give us boldness as ambassadors of His Son, Jesus Christ.

Will you join me toward that end?

Luis Palau
Evangelistic Association
36 Sycamore Road
Amersham
Buckinghamshire HP6 5DR
England

P.S. If you've just read *Radical Renewal*, congratulations. Before you stop reading, however, I encourage you to take a minute to review my comments in 'How to Use This Book', page 14.

To Ponder

1. 'God's goal is to renew both individuals and local churches as part of His overall plan.' What constitutes a renewed local church? To what degree is your church renewed?

2. When you trace it back, revival and church renewal always begin with a small group of Christians who have

experienced brokenness over sin, then confession, cleansing and a fresh walk with the indwelling Christ. Who in your church could make up such a group? Are you already meeting together? If not, when could you begin meeting to pray for a touch of God in your church?

3. 'Ideally, the principles of radical renewal should be presented as part of an overall strategy for church growth.' How could these principles be presented in your church? How could that be a springboard for evangelism and discipleship?

4. 'The biblical principles presented in this book are deep enough to challenge us for a lifetime, yet they're simple enough for most people to understand and apply immediately.' Which principles have you found the hardest to put into practice so far? Which principles have made the most significant impact on your life?

5. 'If you can provoke a crisis in someone's spiritual life, you can drive him or her back to God.' What spiritual crises have you had? How has God used a crisis to drive you back to Himself? Has He used this book in any way?

6. 'God wants to renew His Church in this country and around the world.' What could God do in your church? In your city? In your country? What will it take to see all that happen?

7. 'If God renews you, you won't have a sectarian bone in your body. Or if you do, you'll crucify it.' What does the New Testament teach about the unity of the Body of Christ? What's the basis for that unity?

To Pursue

1. Begin dreaming about what God might want to do in your church. Use your notebook to write down your ideas under the headings of 'renewal', 'evangelism' and 'discipleship'—especially the nurturing of new believers.

2. Use pages 151–152 as an outline for drafting an overall strategy for renewal, evangelism and discipleship in your

church. Write the first draft in your notebook, then type it up and make copies for others to read and discuss with you.

3. If you're a pastor, teacher or home Bible study leader in your church, decide when you could begin presenting the principles of radical renewal to others. If you're not in a leadership position yet, encourage the pastoral staff and elders or deacons at your church to read this book, and then talk to them about presenting these principles to the whole congregation.

4. At the same time, begin praying by name for all the spiritual leaders within your church. Ask the Lord to do a great work in their lives, and to renew the whole church body. Especially ask God to give you greater love for one another.

5. Pray for other churches in your area, too. Begin meeting with people from other churches to pray for a movement of God in your city. If possible, schedule an areawide concert of prayer. But don't stop there. Ask God to renew His Church across this land and around the world for His honour, glory and praise.